To Dick,
With my best wishes
Jim

THE JOHNS HOPKINS UNIVERSITY STUDIES IN HISTORICAL AND POLITICAL SCIENCE

Under the Direction of the Departments of History,
Political Economy, and Political Science

Series LXXX
(1962)

Number 2

THE DECLINE OF THE VENETIAN NOBILITY
AS A RULING CLASS

THE DECLINE OF THE VENETIAN
NOBILITY AS A RULING CLASS

By

JAMES CUSHMAN DAVIS

BALTIMORE
THE JOHNS HOPKINS PRESS
1962

Printed in the United States of America by the J. H. Furst Company

Library of Congress Catalogue Card No. 62-20558

This book has been brought to publication with the assistance
of a grant from the Ford Foundation.

To My Wife,
ELDA

PREFACE

" Decadent " may be too strong a word to apply to the Venice of the seventeenth and eighteenth centuries, but unquestionably there was in this period a many-sided decline of the ancient city-state. There was an obvious loss of political stature; in the early sixteenth century Venice ceased to be a first-rate political power and she ultimately became almost negligible as a force in European affairs. During the sixteenth and early seventeenth centuries there was also a gradual decline of the Venetian economy as Mediterranean trade slowly diminished. In the visual arts too—and Venice had certainly made splendid contributions to the Renaissance—there was a decline, even if there were still the Tiepolos to brighten the eighteenth century.

It was during this same period that the Venetian nobility gradually became inadequate for the responsibilities it had once so gloriously filled: the direction of government, the command of the Venetian navy, and the conduct of Venetian international commerce. (The last was not, of course, exclusively in the hands of noblemen.) The reasons for this inadequacy include among others the economic and demographic decline of the nobility, their loss of public spirit, their more or less conscious imitation of the customs of foreign aristocracies, and the decline in the number of patricians experienced from youth with ships and the sea.

In this study I have concentrated chiefly on the decrease in the size and wealth of the nobility, the effects which these changes had on the ability of this ruling class to conduct the affairs of government, and the creation of new noble families which were made, partly to deal with this problem, in the seventeenth and eighteenth centuries.[1] It should be stressed then that I am deal-

---

[1] There are brief references to one aspect or another of my subject in the following places: John Addington Symonds, *Renaissance in Italy: The Age of Despots* (New York: Holt, 1888), pp. 184-85; " Una delle cause della caduta della repubblica veneta " in *Monumenti storici,* series IV, Miscellanea, Vol. IV (Venice: Deputazione [R.] Veneta di Storia Patria, 1887); Daniele Beltrami, *Storia della popolazione di Venezia dalla fine del secolo xvi alla caduta della Repubblica* (Padua: Cedam, 1954), p. 76; and Ernst Rodenwalt, " Untersuchungen über die Biologie des venezianischen Adels," *Homo Zeitschrift für die Vergleichende Forschung am Menschen,* VIII (1957), I. heft, pp. 1-26. Amintore Fanfani, in " Il mancato rinnovamento economico," *La civiltà veneziana del settecento* (Venice: Centro di cultura e civiltà della fondazione Cini, 1960) has a few pages of observations, largely

9

ing mainly with economic and demographic causes of the governmental problem, and only incidentally with others such as political apathy, and that I am not concerned with the commercial and naval responsibilities of the nobility.

At the end of this book is a brief discussion of some of the implications of this study. It is suggested there that what happened to the Venetian ruling class in the last centuries of the Republic does not only form part of the decline of Venice. Study of it sheds light on some social and political problems then involving most of western Europe, and offers a case study which may interest demographic historians and students of political thought.

To the United States government and the Samuel B. Fels Fund, I am greatly indebted for a Fulbright scholarship and a Fels scholarship. These enabled me to spend a year and a half in Venice doing the research and much of the writing for this study. The Committee on the Advancement of Research at the University of Pennsylvania gave me a grant to cover the cost of preparing the book for publication.

Three students of Venetian history—Professors Gino Luzzatto, Federico Seneca, and Gaetano Cozzi—kindly gave me valuable advice when I began my research, and I would like to thank them for this help. Throughout my work in Venice I had greatly appreciated assistance from the Archivio di Stato's Dr. Ugo Tucci and Dr. Maria Francesca Tiepolo. (In view of the subject of this study, it is interesting to note here that Miss Tiepolo and her mother are the last living members of one of the ancient Venetian noble families.) My brother, Richard P. Davis, and Mrs. Peggy Kerns Band, formerly of The John Hopkins Press, read the manuscript and helped greatly to improve its style, while Professors David Spring, Martin Wolfe, and John F. Benton gave me very useful suggestions regarding both its style and content.

Finally, I would like to thank Professor Frederic C. Lane of The Johns Hopkins University for his help and encouragement from the time when he first introduced me to the study of Venetian history. My debt to him is very great.

inspired by Beltrami's work. In general, these scholars noticed the economic and/or demographic decline of the nobility and hypothesized about possible political results.

CONTENTS

THE DECLINE OF THE VENETIAN NOBILITY
AS A RULING CLASS

CHAPTER I

SIXTEENTH CENTURY BACKGROUND:
THE VENETIAN NOBILITY AS A RULING CLASS

The caste-like nature of the Venetian nobility always looms large in the writings of Renaissance observers of the Republic's constitution.[1] It was natural that they, and later writers too, should find this quality impressive because from the last years of Marco Polo's life until the terrible war with the Turks in the middle of the seventeenth century, the Venetian nobility was remarkable for its policy of exclusiveness. The patricians were organized as a distinct social class with jealously guarded privileges. In order to avoid contamination by inferiors and to keep power in their own hands, they refused to accept new members; they adopted strict rules regarding marriages; and they kept careful birth and marriage records in the famous Golden Books.

But the ruling class had not always had this exclusive character. Most historians now agree that for the first eight centuries after the barbarian invasions and the consequent migrations into the lagoons there was no organized, permanent, and clearly distinguishable "nobility" in the Venetian islands.[2] If the rem-

---

[1] See Gàsparo Contarini, La republica e i magistrati di Vinegia (Venice: Sabini, 1551), trans. from his De magistratibus & republica Venetorum; Donato Giannotti, Libro de la repubblica de Vinitiani (Rome: Blado, 1542); Francesco Guicciardini, Del reggimento di Firenze, in Opere inedite di . . .; illustrate da Giuseppe Canestrini e pubblicate per cura dei conti Pieri e Luigi Guicciardini (10 vols. published as 5; Florence: Cellini, 1857-67).

[2] It would be pointless to list here the many historians who have written on the origins of the Venetian nobility, and their points of view. My summary of this question and the so-called serrata of the Great Council is drawn largely from Roberto Cessi's Le origini del ducato veneziano, Collana Storica IV (Naples: Morano, 1951), Chap. XI; and his essay on the Great Council in Deliberazioni del maggior consiglio di Venezia, in Atti delle assemblee costituzionali italiane dal medio evo al 1831 (3 vols.; Rome: Accademia nazionale dei lincei, Commissione per gli atti delle assemblee costituzionali italiane), Vol. I, Series 3, Sec. 1.

15

nants of the Roman nobility of north Italian cities did flee to the islands along with the other refugees, they did not continue to hold special privileges which set them apart from the others. The *tribuni*, who ruled the Venetian islands before the doge emerged as the principal authority, constituted a kind of *de facto* nobility, but they later disappeared and all that remained of them was a hereditary but purely honorific title attached to the names of some of the families which had once provided tribunes. Of course, there were always groups of men who dominated public affairs, but until the end of the thirteenth century, the doges and other officials who ruled Venice had no exclusive right to rule and belonged to no clearly marked governing class. Their qualifications for office were nothing more nor less than their wealth, ability, and interest in government. While they held office they were known as nobles, but the title derived from the fact of holding office and was temporary. The leading families seem to have dominated the popular assembly, and decrees and pacts were signed by principal citizens.

At the end of the thirteenth century a nobility with definite membership and specific political privileges did finally emerge. The new development is closely related to the history of the Great Council. This body had developed out of a *Consilium sapientum* which was created in 1142 to deal with a temporary situation about which little is known. It remained in existence and gradually became the principal legislative body; it was known as the *Maius Consilium* (the *Maggior Consiglio* or Great Council).[3] The Great Council contained first thirty-five, and later one hundred, elected " ordinary " members, in addition to a much larger number of members who were entitled to take part in it by virtue of being in other offices or councils.

At the end of the thirteenth century the members of the Great Council passed a major constitutional law regarding the membership of this body. It granted membership to all who had belonged to the Great Council at any time in the preceding four years [4] and established a three-man electoral commission which

---

[3] *Maggior* actually means " greater " and implied a comparison with the *Minor Consiglio* which consisted of six ducal councilors and the doge. Historians writing in English usually simplify matters by referring to the *Maggior Consiglio* not as the Greater but as the Great Council.

[4] They had to be approved by the *Quarantia,* a legislative body.

could propose for membership other men who had not belonged to the Council during this time. According to Roberto Cessi, one main purpose of this constitutiontal change was to end the imbalance between ordinary and ex-officio members of the Great Council. Now membership was no longer dependent either on election as one of the one hundred ordinary members or on holding an office which conferred ex-officio membership. All members of the body enjoyed the same status. Another aim of the law was to guarantee membership in the Great Council to all influential Venetians who had established a kind of right to belong to it. During the thirteenth century the Great Council and the various offices of the government were usually filled by men from the same group of families. Many of these men had served so often that they had acquired what was now recognized as almost a right to membership in the Great Council. When, for complicated but purely technical reasons, fewer men were annually elected to the legislative body toward the end of the thirteenth century, a number of influential Venetians found themselves excluded from it. The law of 1296-97 took away any limits on the size of the body and confirmed the right of all men who had previously been active in the government to take part in the Great Council.

This law and those that followed in the next two and a half decades have traditionally been considered a "closing" of the Great Council by a group of men determined to become an exclusive political caste. This was certainly not the original intention. The immediate effect of admitting those who had been temporarily excluded and of providing for election to the Great Council of men who had never taken part in it and had no hereditary claim was not to diminish, but to greatly enlarge, the legislative body. In the following decades, however, the Great Council was indeed "closed." The original willingness to accept new men who were proposed by the electoral commission gradually disappeared, and laws were passed which made the requirements for approval of the proposed men increasingly rigorous.[5] Soon the only new nobles who were accepted were foreign princes

[5] There is a useful account of this legislation in Chapter IX of Francis C. Hodgson, *Venice in the Thirteenth and Fourteenth Centuries* . . . (London: Allen, 1910).

and nephews of popes, who received what amounted to honorary grants of nobility. (As we shall see, however, one major exception was made in 1381.) The dropping of the practice of co-opting new members meant that the Great Council soon became a very exclusive body. At about the same time there was another, almost equally important development. The principle was established that all important government offices must be filled by members of the Great Council.[6] From this time forward, the status of Venetian nobility, membership in the Great Council, and the right to take part in directing the government were synonymous.

Although the laws passed in 1297 and the following years changed the constitution in such a way as to exclude new members, the Great Council made an exception in 1381 and ennobled thirty men who had fought well or contributed money to the cause of the Republic during the War of Chioggia against Genoa.[7] During the wars of the fifteenth and early sixteenth centuries, a few individuals from the mainland of northern Italy who had commanded Venetian mercenary troops were rewarded with membership in the nobility,[8] but they and their families did not play an important part in subsequent Venetian history. The ennoblements of 1381 were the last important exception to the policy of exclusiveness until the middle of the seventeenth century. For 265 years it was virtually impossible for even the wealthiest and most able nonnoble Venetian citizen to enter the ruling class.

From fifteenth-century records it is clear that exclusion of new blood from the nobility was a deliberate policy. In 1403 two of the three presidents of the chief judicial body proposed in the

---

[6] The Venetians never passed a general law reserving important offices for nobles. The constitutional historian Vettore Sandi cites a law of 1478 which reserves certain offices for nobles, but this seems merely to have confirmed a long established practice. *Principi di storia civile della repubblica di Venezia dalla sua fondazione sino all'anno di N. S. 1700* (6 vols.; Venice: Coleti, 1755-56), pt. II, II, pp. 700-701.

[7] Samuele Romanin, *Storia documentata di Venezia* (10 vols.; Venice: Fuga, 1912-21), III, 300-301.

[8] According to a seventeenth-century manuscript in the Marciana library entitled *Distinzioni Segrete che corrono fra le Casate Nobili di Venezia*, there were eight such families. (Biblioteca Nazionale Marciana), It. VII, 2226 (9205). Hereafter all citations beginning with Marc. will refer to manuscripts in the Marciana library.

Pien Collegio, or Cabinet, that the Great Council should accept into the nobility a family from the Venetian middle class (the *cittadini originali*) for every noble family that died out. Presumably their intention was simply to keep the nobility always at full strength and to encourage the virtues of hard work and loyalty in the *cittadini.* But the plan was opposed, ostensibly on a procedural ground, by others in the *Pien Collegio,* and never came under consideration in the Great Council.[9] The same proposal was made again from time to time in the fifteenth century, but always in vain.[10] It is startling to think that if this plan had been adopted the nature of the Venetian nobility would have been different, and the difficult situation which arose in the seventeenth and eighteenth centuries when the ruling class declined in size might have been avoided.

During the fifteenth and sixteenth centuries the nobility gradually perfected the rules designed to preserve the body from contamination. Regulations were established governing marriages with commoners, providing for careful examination of claims to nobility by men who came to Venice from Venetian possessions in the Mediterranean, and ensuring the exclusion of illegitimate sons from noble rights.[11] In 1506 the government began to keep records of the births of noble male citizens and twenty years later it began to record the marriages of all noblemen. These records are in the well-known Golden Books.

Was the exclusiveness of the Venetian nobility unique in early modern Europe? Generally, entrance into the various nobilities and gentries of other states was not easy, but rarely was it impossible. A man of wealth and ability could usually buy the land or the office, or render the service which paved the way to some kind of noble status, if not for himself, then for his descendants. (With the aristocratic reaction of the later seventeenth and eight-

---

[9] Archivio di Stato di Venezia, Pien Collegio, Notatorio (1397-1406), fol. 110v., no. 399, Oct. 24, 1403. Hereafter all citations beginning with the initials A.S.V. will refer to manuscripts in the Archivio di Stato di Venezia.

[10] According to Antonio Battistella, *La Repubblica di Venezia ne' suoi undici secoli di storia* (Venice: Ferrari, 1921), p. 561, similar proposals were made in 1467, 1468 and " più oltre." I could not find records of them in the Notatorio of the Pien Collegio.

[11] Sandi, *Principi di storia civile . . . all'anno di N.S. 1700,* pt. II, I, pp. 273-74; pt. II, II, pp. 699-701; pt. III, I, pp. 11-19.

eenth centuries, many of the aristocracies would become more exclusive.)[12] As another ruling group of a large Italian city-state, the patriciate of Milan provides a meaningful comparison with the Venetian nobility. From the fourteenth to the late seventeenth century it increased from about 200 to nearly 300 families.[13] In politically turbulent Genoa, new families were admitted or forced their way into the nobility until the sixteenth century; subsequently, however, Genoa had a closed aristocracy like that of Venice.[14] What is unique about the exclusiveness of the Venetian nobility is the combination of two things. The nobility became a closed caste at a time (1381) when most other noble groups were to some extent " flexible " and it continued to be a closed group for a very long period of time. Other groups such as the merchant oligarchies of Florence were " closed " at times in the middle ages, but only for brief periods. The Genoese were a virtually closed group for a longer time than was the Venetian nobility, but they began this phase 150 years later.[15] In the sixteenth century there was no other aristocratic group in Europe like the nobility of Venice.

By the sixteenth century, the government which the Venetian ruling class directed had become a very complicated structure. Its complexity was partly the result of a strong Venetian attachment to tradition. Government bodies were rarely abolished, but tended to change their nature as centuries passed. As a result of this process, lines of authority between them were often hazy

---

[12] For discussions of admission to the nobilities of the major European countries see A. Goodwin, ed., *The European Nobility in the Eighteenth Century: Studies of the Nobilities of the Major European States in the pre-Reform Era* (London: Black, 1953), pp. 15-17, 25-27, 34-35, 43-44, 64-67, 100-101, 110-11, 123-37, 140-46, 158, 172-76. On the tendency of governing bodies to become more exclusive see Robert R. Palmer, *The Age of the Democratic Revolution: a Political History of Europe and America, 1760-1800*, vol. I, *The Challenge* (Princeton, N. J.: Princeton University Press, 1959), Chap. II.

[13] J. M. Roberts, " Lombardy " (Goodwin, *European Nobility*, pp. 60-82), pp. 64-65. Under both Spain and Austria, the patricians of Milan were active in the governing of Lombardy.

[14] " Genova," in *Enciclopedia italiana di scienze, lettere ed arti*, 1929-37.

[15] Of the various Italian nobilities, Visconti says, " The nobility had been open to personal valor and talent, but after 1560 it closes, becomes exclusive and proud, and requires difficult proofs for admission to the councils and chivalric orders." (Alessandro Visconti, *L'Italia nell'epoca della controriforma dal 1516 al 1713*, Vol. IV in *Storia d'Italia* [Milan: Mondadori, 1958], p. 62.)

and responsibilities were not always clear. Some bodies absorbed a combination of executive, legislative, and judicial functions. The complexity also resulted from a policy of keeping authority diffused; most responsibility was not in the hands of individuals but of committees of noblemen. (There is a diagram of government offices among the pages of illustrations.)

The important Venetian offices and committees are best pictured as forming a pyramid. I should add, however, that in this pyramid of offices not all power flowed down from the apex or up from the base. At the pinnacle was the splendid, venerable, but almost powerless doge. By the sixteenth century the aristocracy had so reduced the authority of his position that the doge did little but preside over great receptions and council meetings. As the pyramid begins to broaden, we find him joined by six ducal councilors, who assisted the doge and prevented him from acting with any independence. When presiding at certain functions, these seven men were joined by the three chiefs of the *Quarantia Criminale,* the highest judicial body.

Below this group came the *Collegio,* or College of Sages, which was really a committee of the Senate. This body included six *savi grandi,* who took turns heading the affairs of the *Collegio;* five *savi di terra ferma,* who were in charge of affairs on the Venetian mainland; and five *savi ai ordeni,* young men in charge of maritime affairs but in the *Collegio* mainly to learn the arts of administration. When the doge, ducal councilors, chiefs of the *Quarantia Criminale,* and *Collegio* joined, they formed the full or *Pien Collegio.* This body met almost daily to discuss and arrange all business which was to be laid before the Senate for approval. The Senate, partly elected by the Great Council but also including *ex officio* members, comprised about 300 noblemen. Most of the Republic's important affairs were managed by Senate committees and voted on by the body as a whole.

At the base of the pyramid was the Great Council. Every nobleman over twenty-five years of age belonged to this council, and it appears that most of those who were not out of the city for reasons of business or pleasure attended its regular meetings every Sunday. If the *Pien Collegio* was the initiative and executive body, and the Senate was the legislative, the Great Council was the electoral member. While it did have the privilege of approving constitutional changes, its most time-consuming duty was the election of nobles to a great number of government offices.

Off to one side was the powerful Council of Ten, whose authority was never greater than in the sixteenth century. This body's original mandate to deal with matters affecting the security of the state had been very loosely interpreted and the Ten took a hand in all important functions of the government. After 1539 the Council of Ten chose three inquisitors of state (two from its midst) and entrusted them with particularly secret affairs. Also outside of the pyramid framework were the three judicial bodies, each composed of forty members, known as the *Quarantie*. Finally, there were the ambassadors and governors. By the sixteenth century Venice had ambassadors in residence at all times in Rome, Vienna, Madrid, Paris, and Constantinople. There were noble governors in most of the cities and islands under her control, with two of them in each of the more important cities.

The offices and committees named above are only the most important. Altogether, there were roughly 800 government positions (the number varies from century to century) to be filled by patricians. It was possible to hold more than one of the less important posts, however, so that there were perhaps 400 or 500 nobles holding offices at any one time. Many of these offices were sinecures, designed primarily to provide a living for the poorer noblemen.[16]

It is difficult to say just how many very capable noblemen were needed to fill the most important positions. One reason for the difficulty is that it is not easy to say which were key posts. One might question, for example, whether the three *avogadori del comun*, who might be described as official constitutional author-

---

[16] According to the seventeenth-century nobleman, Giannantonio Muazzo, "Numerous profitable offices provide for many the means to support their families." (*Storia del governo antico e presente della Repubblica di Venezia*, MS, Marc. It. VII, 966 [8406]. For a discussion of Muazzo and his writings see Critical Note 3.) The office of *apontador a San Marco* is an example of a Venetian sinecure. According to Sanuto, the *apontador* was usually an old, poor noble who checked attendance in certain paid offices each day and found replacements for those who were absent, receiving fees from the substitutes. (*Cronachetta di Marino Sanuto*, ed. Rinaldo Fulin [Venice: Visentini, 1880], p. 178.)

ities, belonged in the inner circle. They had previously been very important, but seem to have lost their authority while that of the Council of Ten increased. Some posts, such as the governorships of a few mainland cities, were "important" partly because they were hard to fill; they required men with enough wealth to live in a suitably splendid manner. Another difficulty in counting the men in the ruling nucleus is that it is hard to tell just how many capable nobles, at any given time, were temporarily out of office. A *savio grande*, for instance, could not have two successive six-month terms in that office. In the six-month period of *contumacia* after one term as a *savio*, he might simply attend Senate meetings or he might be assigned to a lesser office. There must have been a fairly large number of men at all times who had just finished terms of office and were waiting to be elected to new posts.

If we count the members of the *Pien Collegio*, and add the Council of Ten, the five resident ambassadors, the governors of leading cities and islands, the members of a few principal Senate committees, and a few naval officers, it appears that at any one time there were about sixty noblemen filling key positions. Adding to these another forty men who might have been temporarily inactive because their terms of office had expired, or they were sick, traveling, or attending to business affairs, the total goes up to about 100. In other words, to have an efficiently run government it was necessary to have about 100 men with the wealth, ability, and public spirit which would qualify them for principal offices as administrators, legislators, governors, judges, or ambassadors. These 100 men were the nucleus of the ruling class.

In the first half of the sixteenth century there were over 2,500 noblemen of office-holding age [17] from which to choose the 100-odd men needed for key positions. While this was a fairly large number, it goes without saying that many noblemen were active in trade or lacked the necessary ability or interest to be useful members of the government. In order to make its numbers suffice for the many important offices, the nobility had developed several expedients. One of the most interesting of these was the

[17] One could hold office after reaching the age of twenty-five. On the number of Venetian noblemen in the sixteenth, seventeenth, and eighteenth centuries, see Chapter III.

use of members of the Venetian middle class—the *cittadini originali*—to flesh out the bureaucracy. The *cittadini* were a little more numerous than the nobility.[18] They are sometimes referred to as the secretary class, although being a *cittadino* entitled one not only to serve the government, but also to participate in foreign trade. Over 100 *cittadini* served the government in fairly important functions. Most of these were committee secretaries, archivists, and what might be called staff members of the *Collegio*. The latter, according to Romanin, studied administrative problems, made reports to the Senate, and drew up decrees.[19] From the ranks of the *cittadini* who served in these various posts were chosen the secretaries of ambassadors and the government's ministers in Turin, Milan, Naples, and London. There was another group of *cittadini* of a somewhat inferior rank who served as notaries, fiscal lawyers, and accountants in lesser government bodies.

While Venetian noblemen usually held their government posts for periods of only six months or a year, the *cittadino* committee secretaries and staff members were likely to serve in the same offices for decades. Their experience and knowledge of routine undoubtedly made them indispensable to the constantly changing membership of noblemen. The same thing may have been true in embassies. There is a suggestion of the valuable service the *cittadini* rendered in a little essay on the Venetian government which was written in 1580 by a leading member of this bureaucratic class.[20] The writer says that he who serves as secretary in a government office should study the laws regarding that office, keep secret what is secret, pay attention to everything, keep clear

[18] Daniele Beltrami, *Storia della popolazione di Venezia dalla fine del secolo XVI alla caduta della Repubblica* (Padua: Cedam, 1954), p. 72. According to Beltrami, in 1581, the nobility made up 4.5 percent of the Venetian population, while the *cittadini* comprised 5.3 percent.

[19] See Romanin, *Storia documentata*, VIII, pp. 389-94, on the offices held by *cittadini originali*.

[20] *Ragionamento di doi gentil'homini l'uno Romano, l'altro Venetiano. Sopra il governo della Rep.ca Venetiana, fatto alli 15. di Gennaro, 1580. al modo di Venetia* MS, Marc. It. VII, 709 (8403), fols. 48-50v. This essay is to be found in a manuscript which also contains a "discourse" purportedly written by the grand chancellor, Antonio Milledonne. As both essays bear the same date and are in the same handwriting, and because of a reference to Milledonne in *Ragionamento*, I suspect that he is the author of both works.

and full notes, and in his minutes of meetings summarize both points of view expressed in the discussions. "And because sometimes the gentlemen cannot keep all affairs in mind, the secretary will take care to remind them, not publicly but apart, always with modesty and respect, and often he will prepare and make notes of things which do not require consultation, so that they can be expedited more quickly." It seems likely that these permanent middle class civil servants enabled the nobles to "spread themselves thin" in the administration of the state.

Another method of making the available number of qualified noblemen suffice for the key posts was to require all men elected to offices to accept their assignments. Actually this practice dated from the late twelfth-century when the Republic first decreed penalties for refusals to serve in some positions. As it expanded its functions in the following centuries, the government needed more men to serve on its busy committees and increasingly used the threat of fines and banishments to obtain them.[21] It raised the number of offices which involved penalties if refused and increased the penalties by also temporarily excluding the recalcitrants from the Great Council, the Senate, and the *Quarantie*.[22] These devices had the effect of forcing members of the ruling class to subordinate, temporarily at least, their own interests to those of the state.

This ruling class was distinctive in many ways, not the least of which was the capacity of its members to co-ordinate their efforts to achieve a common purpose. This ability was most evident in public life and it is reflected in the comparative rarity of major disputes within the nobility, the constant adherence to constitutional practices, and the fact that so few individual men ever seem to have so dominated Venetian affairs that they became famous in their own right. The same ability to co-ordinate efforts was seen, but less obviously, within Venetian families. In Venice, it was the class or the family, not the individual, that predominated. Yet, because families and classes are composed of individuals, it seems useful to sketch the career of a typical

[21] Vittorio Lazzarini, "Obbligo di assumere pubblici uffici nelle antiche leggi veneziane," *Archivio Veneto*, XIX (1936), pp. 184-91.
[22] See A.S.V., Comp. leggi, b. 198, which contains legislation on refusals of offices.

sixteenth-century nobleman in order to provide a background for an understanding of matters discussed in the following chapters.[23]

A typical nobleman would have borne the name of a family which actually had clan-like characteristics. Numerous branches of the family might occupy palaces in different parts of the city; some of these might be closely related to the nobleman, while others would be so distant in kinship and degree of wealth that he would have little or no contact with them. In the palace where he lived there might be three or four generations of his own branch of the family. Unmarried brothers and sisters would have their own apartments in the palace on upper floors, while a brother who had married lived with his family in rooms on the second or third floor, which was known as the *piano nobile*. Thus the living arrangements were a physical expression of the ability for co-ordinated effort which characterized the nobility.

Young noblemen were frequently educated at home by private teachers, although there were some academies for wealthy children. Some boys were sent to schools in other parts of Italy, and if our nobleman was studiously inclined, he might eventually be sent to the University of Padua. But for the majority of boys, their more formal education soon merged into training for the business of their fathers.

In Venice the family partnership or *fraterna* was the dominant form of business organization. Under Venetian law, members of a family that lived together and did business as a unit automatically became full partners. Usually all property inherited from the father was entered on the account books of the *fraterna*. Expenditures for food and household furnishings, as well as business expenses, were recorded in the ledger along with the sales and purchases of merchandise.[24] Quite evidently this was an organization which demanded a high degree of co-ordination of effort within the family and agreement as to family aims. Young noblemen frequently participated in the family's business affairs at the

[23] Charles E. Yriarte, *La vie d'un patricien de Venise au seizième siècle* (Paris: Plon, 1874) is an interesting biography of a wealthy nobleman. Yriarte's aim, like mine in this sketch, was to illustrate the nature of a class. His subject, however, was not interested primarily in government affairs.

[24] Frederic C. Lane, "Family Partnerships and Joint Ventures in the Venetian Republic," *Journal of Economic History*, IV (1944), No. 2, pp. 178-96.

ages of fifteen or sixteen and could qualify for trading voyages even at that early age. A will which one noble merchant drew up at the beginning of the sixteenth century is illustrative. He instructed his executors to allot up to 500 ducats to each of his three sons when he reached the age of sixteen so that he might use it on a galley voyage to Alexandria or Beirut. This would serve, of course, to initiate the boy into the family enterprise. He begged the three boys to remain united as a *fraterna* because they would live " with more love, with more honor, with less expense, and with greater profit." [25]

The boy who in this way began his business career might be given some political instruction during the same period of his life. If a father or uncle was elected ambassador or governor of a subject city or island, the boy might well be taken along. This would give him an excellent opportunity to learn how to represent his state or govern her subject territories. Then, sometime between the ages of twenty and twenty-five, he could be chosen by lot to enter the Great Council—otherwise he would enter automatically at the age of twenty-five—and could begin his political education in earnest. A promising young man was often made *savio ai ordeni* as soon as he entered the Great Council; this put him in the *Collegio* where he could learn the arts of administration under older, experienced men. Later a young noble might be elected to other committee positions that entitled him to attend Senate meetings. The Senate was a school of public affairs for the younger men, not only because they could therein observe the daily conduct of public business, but because ambassadors and governors who returned to Venice from their posts were required to come to the Senate and read reports— which were often interesting and perceptive—on what they had seen and done on their tours of duty.

There were two major careers open to most Venetian noblemen: one was in trade and the other in public service. But it was not always necessary to choose between them. The young nobleman portrayed here might be initiated into business during his teens and continue to go on voyages for many years, but even if he traveled and resided abroad for as many as twenty years

[25] Will of Gabriel Barbarigo, A.S.V., *Testamenti notarili*, 1229, no. 125, fol. 105v.

before he returned to Venice, he would still be only in his mid-thirties at the end of this period. For the rest of his life he could combine business and political activities or give up the former and concentrate on serving the state. The nature of Venetian business was such that some men with very active political careers could still keep a hand in trade. Andrea Gritti was well into middle age and had made himself rich as a grain trader in Istan-bul before he returned to Venice at the start of the sixteenth cen-tury. In the next two decades he became successively ducal coun-cilor, civilian commander-in-chief of the Venetian armies, ambas-sador to France, and doge. We know from a contemporary diary that when Gritti was elected doge he took grain from his ware-house and, to celebrate his victory, sold it at a price far below the market level. In all of these political years he had not aban-doned his trading activities.[26]

There were unquestionably some young men from wealthy families who concentrated exclusively on political careers, just as there were others who never took an active part in the govern-ment. Here again the Venetian family tradition of co-ordination of efforts played a part. Political, business, and other activities were often allotted to or assumed by different brothers in a fam-ily according to their interests. Thus a nobleman at the end of the sixteenth century wrote in his will that he had destined his second son to trade, and he urged his older son " who, if I am not mistaken, appears to be inclined toward letters," to live a stu-dious life and spend whatever money was necessary for the pur-pose.[27] A contemporary of the outstanding seventeenth-century Venetian statesman, Battista Nani, said that Divine Providence had given Nani a brother who could capably manage the family finances. This arrangement freed Battista to devote all of his tal-ents to the government.[28]

Needless to say, a successful political career in Venice was almost impossible for a nobleman without a fair amount of wealth. Only a man of means could pay for a good education

---

[26] Marino Sanuto, *I diarii*, eds.: Rinaldo Fulin, Nicolò Barozzi, Guglielmo Ber-chet, Marco Allegri (58 vols., Venice: Deputazione [R.] veneta di Storia Patria, 1879-1903), XXXIV, col. 184.
[27] Will of Antonio Maria Bernardo, A.S.V., *Testamenti notarili,* 1249, t. II, fol. 110.
[28] *Relazione del anonimo,* p. 387. (For full citation see Critical Note 3.)

for his sons, and a well-trained mind was, then as now, a prime requisite for a good administrator.[29] The son of a wealthy man was also likely to have the advantage of seeing at first hand how an ambassadorial mission was performed. Later on, his own riches would enable him to serve as ambassador or governor; poorer men could not afford these posts because the expenses often greatly exceeded the stipends.[30] In a subtle way, too, wealth conferred the prestige which helped men reach the most important offices. Along with influential relatives and numerous friends, wealth made up the " Tripod of Venetian success." [31]

For a young man with political ambitions, there were recognized routes leading upward through the bewildering maze of committees, governorships, embassies, and judicial bodies. Most states have had such chains of offices, one of the best known being the *cursus honorum* of the Romans. (Fortunately for the Venetian noblemen, they were not required at any point to provide anything equivalent to bread and circuses, though some posts called for expensive living.) The purpose of these ladders of offices, in Venice as elsewhere, was to enable men to move by measured paces from less demanding posts to more important ones, gaining experience as they progressed. It appears that there were five chief routes open to young Venetian noblemen.

One route led through the governorships. A man following this path might begin in one of the very minor mainland posts, then govern the relatively unimportant city of Vicenza, return to Venice to serve for a time in one of the offices which gave temporary membership in the Senate, then serve perhaps at Bergamo, follow this with more important duties in Venice, and

[29] One seventeenth-century writer said that the poor nobles in the Great Council were " without any personal ability, because their Fathers had no means to have them taught . . ." (*Relazione della Serenissima Repubblica*, MS, p. 115. For a full citation of this work, see Critical Note 3.)

[30] When doge Francesco Erizzo, whose political career began in the last decade of the sixteenth century, made up his will in 1635, he set aside a house near Mestre and one hundred fields, the income from which was to go to his oldest nephew to help with expenses he might incur while in the service of the government outside Venice. The nephew was to use half of the income to help his brothers when they were serving " in some honorable Governorship or other Office abroad." (A.S.V., *Testamenti notarili*, 1140, t. I, fol. 43.) The date of the will falls outside of the sixteenth century, but it illustrates as well as anything could the necessity of wealth for a distinguished political career.

[31] *Esame Istorico Politico*, MS, p. 91. (For full citation, see Critical Note 3.)

then go to Verona or one of the more important maritime governorships on Crete or elsewhere. He might then become *savio grande* or a member of the Council of Ten; only at that point was he considered experienced enough to govern the cities of Brescia and Padua.[32]

The ambassadorial route involved a hierarchy of capital cities. At the bottom were temporary embassies in Savoy or the Netherlands,[33] followed by France or Spain, and then Vienna or Rome or Constantinople. Although the order of importance was roughly fixed, rarely would a man serve in all of these capitals. Between embassies he would serve in various posts of increasing importance in Venice.

A third route led through the committees of the *Collegio.* Here a young man would almost invariably start as one of the five *savi ai ordeni.* His next major goal would be *savio di terra ferma,* followed after many years by the position of *savio grande.* There were two other generally recognized sequences of offices —in the field of law and on the sea—but fewer men reached the highest positions by means of them. Probably naval commands had had more political importance when Venice was a greater sea power. For all of the routes, the goal was to enter the inner circle of *savi grandi,* ducal councilors, and members of the Council of Ten. These men strove in turn to be among the nine procurators of St. Mark—a largely honorary post—and ultimately doge.

There was a great deal of overlapping between the various routes of offices. The career of one man might easily include embassies, governorships, and positions in the *Collegio.* And, of course, there was great variety in the timing and degree of success among men who rose through these offices. Men who were not primarily interested in government affairs might alternate important posts with minor ones;[34] this was true even of some

[32] *Relazione della Serenissima,* pp. 110-11. Much of my information comes from this and from the *Esame Istorico Politico.* These treatises on the Venetian government date from the seventeenth century, but the writers carefully distinguish between the former ladders of office and the changed routes which existed in their times. In any case, the existence of these routes, essentially as described here, will be familiar to anyone who has read Venetian biographies, lists of men's offices, etc.

[33] *Esame Istorico Politico,* pp. 13-14.

[34] An example is Marc' Antonio Barbaro, subject of Yriarte's *La vie d'un patricien.*

leading statesmen. Sometimes a man of great ability, like Andrea Gritti who was mentioned earlier, began an active political career fairly late in life but rose rapidly to the top.

If the hypothetical nobleman under discussion here reached the important offices, he had to be ready to devote most of his time to public service. Members of the *Pien Collegio* met almost every morning, and twice on the many days when the Senate held its meetings. All of the important members of the government attended the Senate meetings and those of the Great Council, in addition to those of committees to which they belonged. At any time they might be elected ambassadors and sent out of Venice for periods of three years. Their service in the government, furthermore, might last from their twenties or thirties until death. Many important members of the government were in their seventies and eighties.

Two sixteenth-century noblemen, Marino Sanuto and Leonardo Donà, together give an idea of the best qualities of the ruling class. Sanuto belonged to a very old, once powerful family, but poor management of the estate by one of his brothers had cost them nearly all of the patrimony. Marino was occasionally a *savio ai ordeni,* held a few other minor posts, and once in a while became a senator, but he never held any important offices. Yet he was ambitious, deeply devoted to the state (as his well-known 58-volume diary shows), and greatly respected for his knowledge of Venetian law and custom and his insistence on observing them. It was probably his frankness and vehement, and almost pedantic insistence on legality which offended others and kept him from winning important positions for which he felt qualified, or prevented him from gaining support for his proposals in the Senate. In his diaries he frequently expresses disappointment over his lack of success and talks of giving up public life, but his affection for the Republic always won out. He had his consolation in writing Dante-like imprecations on his enemies — " Anyone who does not want me in the Senate would make an enemy of God and the Republic "—and knowing that his name was something of a byword for legality and constitutionalism among the nobles.[35]

[35] Mario Brunetti, " Marin Sanudo (profilo storico)," *Ateneo Veneto,* Vol. 1923, pp. 51-67.

The success of Leonardo Donà's career contrasts with the relative failure of Sanuto's. Donà was born in 1536, the year Sanuto died. Even before he entered active political life he formed the habit of studying assiduously Venetian law and the practice of government. For example, among his papers conserved in the library of the Correr Museum there is a 200-page " Summary of the laws and decrees pertaining to the [Venetian] Kingdom of Cyprus and to its royal council, composed by me Leonardo Donato, with no little diligence and effort, reading the books of the Royal Chancellery, in the year 1557, the twenty-second [year] of my youth, while I was with the illustrious Sig.r Giobatta Donato my father, of respected memory, Lieutenant Governor in the said Kingdom . . ." [36] For almost all of the offices he held, Donà made careful studies of their capitularies, the laws relating to them, and reports made by men who had previously served in them. These compilations fill many volumes among the Donà papers. Even among the leading Venetian statesmen, Donà was considered outstanding for his continual self-instruction, his austere dedication to the government, his eloquence, and his concern with instructing younger men in the art of governing.[37]

Granted that Donà was exceptional, it remains true that the Venetian government needed at least 100 men in the most important offices who reflected similar qualities. During Donà's youth, as I have already said, the Venetian nobility included over 2,500 men of office-holding age from which to choose this core of the ruling class.[38] There seems to have been no major problem in recruiting. Occasionally an ambassador would make a plea for a dispensation from service, as Zaccaria Contarini did in 1500 when he was elected ambassador extraordinary to Hungary, but Contarini could point to his ten children, his sick wife, his previous service on ten embassies (three of them across the Alps), exposure to the dangers of plague on one mission in Germany, and the fact that his father and two other relatives had died of

[36] Biblioteca del Museo Correr, Donà 46. Hereafter all citations beginning with the word Correr will refer to manuscripts in the Correr library.
[37] Federico Seneca, Il doge Leonardo Donà: La sua vita e la sua preparazione politica prima del dogado, (Padua: Antenore, 1959).
[38] See Chapter Three.

the rigors of serving as ambassadors.[39] In general, the government could recruit enough qualified men. Registers show that the "nominators" almost always managed to find the required number of men to propose as candidates for important offices.[40] There is very little legislation on the subject of refusals of offices during most of the sixteenth century, and the tone of the preambles to what laws were passed does not suggest that refusals were a serious problem.[41] Furthermore, the diaries of Sanuto and the essays on the constitution by Giannotti and Contarini do not mention any difficulty in finding enough men for offices. Apparently the ruling class was large enough to provide enough men of good calibre for the government.

[39] G. R. Potter (ed.), *The New Cambridge Modern History*, Vol. I, *The Renaissance 1493-1520* (Cambridge: University Press, 1957), p. 272.

[40] Marc., It. VII, pp. 813-71 (8892-8930). The registers begin with the year 1498 and are complete almost until 1797. Each volume covers a period of about five years. The Archivio di Stato di Venezia possesses a similar set of registers.

[41] See the collection of laws on refusals cited earlier: A.S.V., Comp. leggi, b. 198.

CHAPTER II

THE NOBILITY BECOMES POORER

In most societies families move constantly from one class into another. Even though the character of any particular class may persist, the roster of its families is likely to change very much over a century or two. This process usually takes place without any ceremony. When a particular family in one class changes in such a way as to have the qualities of families in another, it moves up or down across the class border line. In discussing this process, Joseph Schumpeter offers the example of the German high nobility during the Middle Ages. A family was tacitly accepted in this class if it achieved great wealth, success, and prestige; if it lost these, it lost its place in the nobility.[1] In some societies law or custom has conferred specific distinctions such as political or religious privileges on members of a class; then there may be a recognizable ceremony when a family enters the group. Even in these cases, the act of admission does not move the family across a class borderline; it merely formalizes what has become an obvious fact.

The Venetian nobility thwarted this process. It did this by adopting a policy of rigid exclusiveness and sticking to it for two and a half centuries. From the fourteenth century to the middle of the seventeenth, as was seen in Chapter I, the Venetians did not confer nobility even upon the wealthiest, most decorous and most loyal of the nonnoble families. Entrance was thus blocked for those wealthy and able men of the middle class who might constantly have replenished the nobility. The Venetians also thwarted the natural process of movement across class lines because they, like most contemporary nobilities, treated noble sta-

[1] Joseph A. Schumpeter, "Social Classes in an Ethnically Homogeneous Environment," an essay reprinted in *Imperialism; Social Classes* (New York: Sweezy, 1951); Heinz Norden, trans., the chapter, "Movement across Social Lines."

tus as a permanent attribute, as hard to lose as it was to gain.
Those families which had belonged to the nobility by 1381 remained permanently in that class. Come what might—poverty,
obscurity, disgrace—they could not lose the indelible character
of nobility. A family left the patriciate only by dying out.[2]

These membership policies prepared the way for some striking changes in the size and wealth of the nobility. These changes
began, or became particularly obvious, after the middle of the
sixteenth century. Having reached what was probably its maximum size, the nobility began to shrink very rapidly. Many of
the smaller families that had played their roles in Venetian history for centuries disappeared completely, while larger ones with
numerous branches were sharply reduced in size. At the same
time (and the two developments were closely related), the number of wealthy nobles decreased. It is the latter change which will
be considered first, in this chapter. In the next chapter we will
turn to the general demographic decline of the nobility.

During the last three centuries of the Republic, the number
of men with enough great wealth to take an important part in
the government apparently diminished sharply. How many of
these men there were will be discussed in some detail later. The
principal reason for the decline seems to have been that families
which became impoverished for any reason during this period—
mismanagement, too many dowries to pay, luxurious living, bad
luck—no longer had the opportunity to rebuild their wealth in
the ancient patrician activity of overseas trade.

It was in this economic field that Venice had excelled during
the Middle Ages. Her geographic position enabled her to profit
enormously by carrying spices and other luxuries from the East
to her own warehouses for subsequent sale to European countries, exporting European wools and silks and gold, carrying
wheat from the Black Sea, wine from the Mediterranean islands,
and so on. Her galley voyages to Syria, to England, to Flanders,
are early examples of large-scale economic enterprises. By law
and by custom, most of this international trade was in the hands
of Venetian noblemen.[3]

---

[2] A few families were banished permanently because members had committed serious crimes.

[3] For an interesting discussion of the economic opportunities available to nobles,

Certainly not all noblemen were rich during this period. But opportunity existed for a man with a small amount of capital to enrich himself. Lane has shown how Andrea Barbarigo, son of a disgraced noble who had been ruined with a crushing fine of 10,-000 ducats, restored his family's wealth. Andrea began with a capital of only two hundred ducats. He took advantage of the opportunity provided by Venice for poor young nobles to sail on merchant galleys as "bowmen of the quarterdeck." Voyages of this kind offered a valuable commercial and maritime apprenticeship, during which Andrea may have made profitable investments with his small capital. He also served in the legal apprenticeship afforded by lucrative, minor posts as official attorney in commercial courts. But Venice did not offer opportunity to young nobles only in these ways. Born in a group with strong commercial traditions, Andrea had relatives and in-laws, and merchant and banker friends who were able and willing to help him. The nature of Venetian commerce, furthermore, made it possible for a man with Andrea's small funds to make many petty investments until he had enough capital to become a fairly important wholesale merchant. When Barbarigo died in 1449, he left an estate of between 10,000 and 15,000 ducats, a substantial amount, although not a fortune in that day.[4]

Their favored position, their skill, and their opportunities for profitable trade certainly brought wealth to the Venetian nobility. Most of the men of wealth in Venice were of this class, and there seems to be no reason to believe that this situation changed until perhaps the seventeenth century. A list of Venetians who were subject to a forced loan in 1379 gives a good basis for a comparison of the nobles' wealth with that of other Venetians. On the list are the names of men with wealth of more than 300 lire, and their declared patrimonies. The patricians on the list outnumber the others by 1,209 to 919. If only those with incomes of over 1,000 lire are considered, the nobles outnumber other Venetians by 780 to 376.[5] Quite obviously, most wealth

and their economic hegemony in Venice, see Gino Luzzatto, "Les activités économiques du patriciat vénitien (x^e-xive siècles)," *Studi di storia economica veneziana* (Padua: Cedam, 1954).

[4] Frederic C. Lane, *Andrea Barbarigo: Merchant of Venice* (Baltimore: The Johns Hopkins Press, 1944), pp. 11-33.

[5] Luzzatto, "Les activités économiques," pp. 134-36.

was in the hands of patricians. And two years later thirty of the wealthiest *cittadini,* who had made large gifts to the Republic to help with war expenses, were ennobled.[6] It would appear that by this time about seventy percent of the wealthy Venetians were nobles. As explained in Chapter I, after this year there were no more creations of nobles until the seventeenth century. The Venetian nobility, therefore, began the 265-year phase of its existence in which it was a closed caste as a body comprising a good majority of the rich men of the city.[7]

If one keeps in mind that the wealth of the nobility was founded on foreign commerce, he can readily see how events of the sixteenth century reduced the economic opportunities from which Andrea Barbarigo had benefited in the preceding century. The first blow was the Portuguese competition in the spice trade which followed the discovery of the route to the East around the southern tip of Africa. From about 1500 to 1530—probably longer, but the picture is not clear—the Venetian spice trade suffered badly.[8] By 1550 a revival seems to have taken place, and the spice trade regained or surpassed its fifteenth-century level. For two or three decades Venetian merchants again prospered.[9]

[6] Their contributions to the government are described in a document published by Vittorio Lazzarini at the end of " Le offerte per la guerra di Chioggia e un falsario del quattrocento," *Nuovo Archivio Veneto* n.s., IV, (1902), pp. 202-13.

[7] Luzzatto (" Les activités économiques," p. 136) believes there were at the time of the forced loan a " good number " of nobles who were not required to lend money because their patrimonies were less than 300 lire. Assuming that the total number of noblemen at that time was about 2,000, and subtracting 1,200 who made loans, it appears there may have been as many as 800 nobles we can describe as poor (with patrimonies of less than 300 lire). But even this figure may be high, since probably some of the 800 men not on the list were wealthy men who were not taxed because their fathers, not they, were heads of families. Probably the number of poor nobles was roughly a third of the nobility.

[8] See Frederic C. Lane, " National Wealth and Protection Costs," in *War as a Social Institution,* J. D. Clarkson and T. C. Cochran (eds.) (New York: Columbia University Press, 1941); and Vitorino Magalhaes-Godinho, " Le repli véniten et egyptien et la route du Cap 1496-1533," *Éventail de l'Histoire Vivante, hommage à Lucien Febvre [à l'occasion de son 75e anniversaire] par l'amitié d'historians, linguistes, géographes, économistes, sociologues, enthnologues,* (2 vols.; Paris: Colin, 1953), II, pp. 283-300. Luzzatto's " La decadenza di Venezia dopo le scoperte geografiche nella tradizione e nella realtà," *Archivio Veneto,* LIV-LV (1954), pp. 162-81, is an excellent summary of the more recent research on the economic decline of Venice.

[9] Frederic C. Lane, " The Mediterranean Spice Trade (Further Evidence of its Revival in the Sixteenth Century)," *American Historical Review,* XLV (1940), pp.

But the expensive War of Cyprus against the Turks in the early 1570's weakened the economy, and in the following decades the Venetians felt the effect of powerful trading competition from the Dutch and English. In the opinions of Venetians of that time and modern historians, the Republic's overseas trade went into a sharp decline in the 1570's, and in the first decades of the seventeenth century it reached a low point from which it never recovered.[10]

What is of interest here are the implications of this decline in trade for the nobility. Quite obviously it reduced the opportunities for making money. For example, the number of Venetian merchants in Constantinople declined sharply as trade opportunities declined in that city. The *bailo* or Venetian ambassador reported in 1612 that where there had once been eighteen or twenty Venetian firms in Constantinople, there were in his time only five.[11] And the decline in the Levant trade probably affected many more noble families. Just how many men were involved in this commerce in the prosperous decades one cannot say, but Leonardo Donà probably did not exaggerate very much when he reminded the Senate in 1610 that there had been a time when " all were merchants and traded, no family excepted either of nobles

581-90. For some reservations about the revival in Syria, see Ugo Tucci's foreword to his *Lettres d'un marchand vénitien, Andrea Berengo (1553-1556)*, (Paris: S.E.-V.P.E.N., 1957), esp. p. 15.

[10] A.S.V., Senato mar, filza 187, insert 6, report of cinque savi alla mercanzia, 5 July 1610, and adjacent documents. Nicolò Donà, who had traded in the prosperous years, wrote in 1610 that, " This city had a flourishing commerce in all of the levant . . . until the last Turkish war, which begin in the year 1569." (MS, Correr, Donà 24, p. 130. This was evidently a speech to be read in the Senate.) Luzzatto ("La decadenza," pp. 174-81) sees the decline as beginning in about 1570. He believes the Mediterranean had not definitely become a secondary trade route until 1625. Braudel believes the Venetian Levant trade decline may have *begun* by 1580 but does not commit himself on developments after 1600. (Fernand Braudel, *La Méditerranée et le monde Méditerranéen à l'époque de Philippe II*, [Paris: Colin 1949], pp. 442-47). See also F. C. Lane, " Venetian Shipping During the Commercial Revolution." *A.H.R.*, XXXVIII (1933), pp. 219-39. Domenico Sella ("Il declino dell'emporio realtino," *La civiltà veneziana nell'età barocca*, Venice: Centro di cultura e civiltà della fondazione Cini, n.d., pp. 99-121), believes the commercial collapse came only in the first decades of the seventeenth century.

[11] Report of Simon Contarini in *Le relazioni degli stati europei lette al Senato dagli ambasciatori veneziani nel secolo decimosettimo*, Nicolò Barozzi and Guglielmo Berchet (eds.), (10 vols.; Venice: Naratovich, 1856-1878), in volume called *Turchia*, p. 235.

or of *cittadini*; when only the ships and merchants of this land frequented the Levant. . . ." [12] But in the time when Donà was speaking, according to a Senate economic committee, Venetian trade in the Levant was in the hands of only a few men who were having a difficult time.[13] By the end of the eighteenth century there were "hardly any" Venetian firms trading in the Levant; the only substantial one was not operated by a noble family.[14]

During these discouraging final decades of the sixteenth century—marked by ups and downs—numerous Venetian families seem to have withdrawn from trade. The Donà family, referred to above, was active in commerce in the mid-sixteenth century, but gave up not long after the battle of Lepanto in 1571 and devoted their efforts to supervising their mainland properties and taking part in government affairs.[15] In their wills, men who had been active as merchants pledged their heirs not to sell their inheritance in order to use the proceeds as capital for trading,[16] and they occasionally voiced an opinion that commerce was an undependable way to make a ducat. The diary of Francesco da Molin suggests what may have become of many nobles with small means in the latter half of the sixteenth century. Just as Andrea Barbarigo had done 150 years before, da Molin served in his youth as "bowman of the quarterdeck" and later held minor official legal posts. When he was later elected councilor at Crete, he took with him "all of that little capital which I possessed, to see if I could increase my few savings in an honest and honorable way. . . ." Whether he made some small gains or

---

[12] MS, Correr, Donà 24, pp. 140-45. (The speech can be found in Romanin, *Storia documentata,* VIII, 530). This Leonardo Donà was the nephew of the doge with the same name.

[13] A.S.V., Senato mar, filza 187, insert 6, report of cinque savi alla mercanzia, July 5, 1610. Insert 5 is a list dated 1610 of 83 noblemen who "have trade in the Levant," but I suspect this includes many men who were not active in commerce in that year.

[14] Speech of Andrea Tron, inquisitore alle arti, in the Senate, March 9, 1784, in Romanin, *Storia documentata,* IX, p. 93. Romanin cites A.S.V., Inquisitorato alle arti, p. 8.

[15] Gaetano Cozzi, *Il doge Nicolò Contarini, Ricerche sul patriziato veneziano agli inizi del Seicento* (Venice: Istituto per la collaborazione culturale, 1958), p. 18.

[16] Aldo Stella, "La crisi economica nella seconda metà del secolo XVI," *Archivio Veneto,* LVIII-LIX (1956), p. 29.

not, he never says, but the 1570's were not promising times. He never mentions business again. After his return from Crete, he concentrated on winning the friends necessary for election to minor salaried offices and in 1577 was very happy to win a place in the *Quarantia* (law court). Commerce seems to have provided him with no living. The opportunities open 150 years earlier to Andrea Barbarigo were largely gone. Like so many of the nobles of modest means, Molin became dependent on public offices for an income.[17]

The withdrawal of many nobles from trade was partly forced by declining opportunities but it was also in part voluntary. The son of Andrea Barbarigo seems only to have dabbled in trade; Andrea's grandsons devoted themselves mainly to political careers; and a great-grandson liquidated the family colonial estates in Crete, bought properties on the mainland, and made no investments in overseas trade. As this took place before the sharp decline in trade which started in the 1570's, it cannot be said that it was the result of that decline; it simply reflects a lack of interest in commerce on the part of men who could live off their income from investments and land.[18] There seems to have been a trend in this direction, which became stronger after Venetian commerce went into a marked decline. At the beginning of the seventeenth century, Leonardo Donà spoke of the way "the nobility wants no part in trade."[19] And 150 years later Andrea Tron made a ringing denunciation of this apathy. He pointed out to his fellow senators that by not being active in commerce nobles deprived the state of revenues and its people of work and set a bad example to the nonnoble Venetian merchants. "It is surprising," Tron said, "how a civilized man can suppose that the military profession, which destroys populations, should entitle one to nobility, while trade, which erases barbarism and replaces it with the arts and sciences, stains the quality of nobility. . . ." No one should think, he went on, that "our ancestors of old times, who certainly deserve as much esteem as

[17] *Compendio delle cose, che riputò degne di tenersi particolar memoria, e che successero dal mese di Aprile 1558 . . . sino all'anno 1598*, MS, Marc., It. VII, 553 (8812). See esp. pp. 10-11, 47, 49.

[18] Lane, *Andrea Barbarigo*, pp. 33-41.

[19] Romanin, *Storia documentata*, VII, p. 530.

we " had not been mindful of their quality and dignity when they engaged in trade. As a contemporary good example he pointed to the Netherlands, where the same men who directed the government were the principal merchants, and the wealth of the most outstanding families was the product and at the same time the producer of a widespread commerce.[20] The attitude which Tron denounced has its physical expression in the magnificent palaces which some noblemen built in the seventeenth and eighteenth centuries. They are sometimes offered as proof that commerce was still flourishing at that time in Venice, but on the contrary they were more probably built with capital no longer used in trade, and they might better be considered the emblems of a feeling that a life of ease and magnificence was more befitting a nobleman than a life devoted to business. A similar distaste for trade was becoming typical of the upper classes in many parts of the Mediterranean world.[21]

The patricians found no substitute for overseas trade in the rising industry that partially compensated Venice for its decline in foreign commerce. Wool manufacturing increased throughout the sixteenth century and reached its peak from 1560 to 1620, at the same time that such luxury industries as silk production had a boom.[22] The Venetian book publishing business also reached its peak during the sixteenth century.[23] But industry was an economic field in which Venetian nobles, by tradition, were not very active. The only important exception was shipbuilding, and this was an activity in sharp decline.[24] The nobles seem to have neglected opportunities to profit by the booming indus-

[20] *Ibid.*, IX, pp. 97-98.
[21] See Braudel, *La Méditerranée*, pp. 616-42.
[22] Domenico Sella, "Les mouvements longs de l'industrie lainière," *Annales Economies Sociétés Civilizations* (1957), pp. 29-45. Dr. Sella kindly told me of the existence of the lists of wool manufacturers referred to below, as well as the documents mentioned above regarding the number of merchants active in the Levant in 1610.
[23] According to Brown, the Venetian publishing business had its biggest volume of production from 1530 to 1570. After a slump caused by the plague of the 1570's the business recovered well, but then underwent a sharp decline at the end of the century as a result of Church censorship, and was never the same again. (Horatio F. Brown, *The Venetian Printing Press: An Historical Study* [New York: Putnam's, 1891], pp. 97-100, 198.)
[24] F. C. Lane, "Venetian Shipping during the Commercial Revolution," *American Historical Review*, XXXVIII (1933), pp. 219-239.

tries.[25] While some may have invested in the publishing business, for example, none of those listed in a compendium of sixteenth-century publisher's names were noblemen.[26] As for the far more important wool industry, in the years 1609-1673 there were only fourteen nobles who were known as " merchant manufacturers " of wool cloth. This was an insignificant number, as is obvious from the fact that even in the single year 1684, when woolen making had greatly declined, there were still ninety-four nonnoble " merchant manufacturers." By 1781, none of the twenty-two wool manufacturers was a noble.[27]

Landowning was different. There is reason to believe that some of the islanders had from the beginning of Venetian history owned fields on the mainland, and after about 1250 this became somewhat more common, but until roughly 1500 Venetian noblemen seem to have considered farmlands on the *Terra Ferma* merely as safe investments for part of their capital and as sources of food for their households.[28] In the sixteenth century, however, landowning became a much more important activity of the wealthy families. Disillusioned with commerce, the Donàs, Barbarigos, Priulis, and many other wealthy families eagerly bought lands and set about improving them. In the seventeenth and eighteenth centuries, they bought so avidly that the proportion of farmland they owned overshadowed to a great extent that of the small holders.[29] Landowning was different from trading and manufacturing not only because it was a safe investment, but also because it was very much in keeping with what was now regarded as the dignity of a nobleman's life. For a wealthy patri-

[25] It will become clear in Chapter V that there were still opportunities in the seventeenth and eighteenth centuries to make fortunes in the textile industries, local trade, and other activities. Over one hundred wealthy middle class families from Venice or its possessions in the period 1646-1718 paid 100,000 ducats each for the privilege of entering the Venetian nobility.

[26] Ester Pastorello, *Tipografi, editori e librai a Venezia nel secolo xvi* (Florence: Olschki, 1924). There are two or three nobles listed here, but they seem to have been men who commissioned single printings.

[27] A.S.V., Inquisitorato alle arti, b. 45, report of Andrea Tron, June 23, 1781, inserts 3, 4, 5. These are lists of manufacturers.

[28] Luzzatto, " Les activités économiques," pp. 125-41.

[29] Daniele Beltrami, *Saggio di storia dell'agricoltura nella repubblica di Venezia durante l'età moderna*, (Venice and Rome: Istituto per la collaborazione culturale, 1956), pp. 69-70.

cian there was much satisfaction in the possession of broad fields, fine horses, and a Palladian villa on one of the placid rivers of the Veneto.

But land, like industry, failed to provide an economic opportunity for nobles of modest incomes. It was most suited to the needs of families with a large fortune earned in commerce who were content to live on what Beltrami calls " a low but sure income." [30] Even these families failed to make the most of their investment. A plan for large-scale improvement of the Venetian mainland territory was proposed by Alvise Corner in the mid-sixteenth century. But the plan, which called for a combination of state administration and private initiative, failed for lack of cooperation. A few families, indeed, such as the Priuli, achieved spectacular results as they improved their possessions. But the Priuli had been wealthy merchants.[31] Land could not do for a nobleman of modest means in 1600 what commerce had done for Andrea Barbarigo almost two centuries earlier.

With trade declining, and no alternatives in industry or landholding, too many could say, with Jonson's Venetian noble, Volpone,

> . . . I use no trade, no venter;
> I wound no earth with plow-shares, fat no beasts
> To feed the shambles; have no mills for yron,
> Oyle, corne, or men, to grinde 'hem into poulder;
> I blow no subtill glasse; expose no ships
> To threatenings of the furrow-faced sea;
> I turne no moneys, in the publicke banke;
> No usure private—

Unlike Volpone, however, they were not rich men.

If ways to make money were declining, ways to spend it were not. Venetian legislators of the last three centuries sadly compared their contemporaries with their ancestors. The latter, they

[30] *Ibid.*, p. 10. The nobleman, Giannantonio Muazzo, commented in the seventeenth century on the fact that many families had turned from commerce to landholding. He said that because more secure incomes (i.e., from land rents) are always smaller, these families made up in security for what they lost in size of income. *Del Governo Antico*, MS, fol. 70. (For full citation and information about Muazzo's work, see Critical Note 3.)

[31] Stella, *op. cit.*, pp. 30, 66-67.

believed, had been sober, thrifty, hard-working gentlemen, who had carefully saved their ducats out of respect for God and the good of their families. Many men of their own times, they lamented, were recklessly squandering the fortunes earned by the toil of previous generations.[32] The fact is that the first known Venetian statute aimed at controlling luxurious living was passed as early as 1299,[33] and sumptuary laws were passed on several occasions in the fourteenth century. But it was in the fifteenth century that there came rapid changes in clothing styles and the development of new tastes which began seriously to tax the abilities of Venetian legislators to control what they considered excessively luxurious living. Some feeling of what happened in Venice is conveyed by comparing the clothing of men in the older mosaics in Saint Mark's with that worn by the figures in Carpaccio's painting depicting the Saint Ursula legend. Where the former style is somber, the latter is fantastic in color and variety. Some of the exasperation with which the legislators witnessed these changes is obvious in a Senate decree of 1504 which declared that

among all the superfluous and useless expenditures for the purpose of ostentation made by the women of this, our city, the most injurious to the substance of the gentlemen [nobles] and citizens is the constant change made by the women in the form of their clothes. For example, whereas formerly they wore trains to the dresses, the fashion was introduced of wearing the dresses round and without any trains. But in the last few months certain women have begun again to use large and ample trains, trailing on the ground, and without doubt all others will desire to follow their example, if measures be not taken, and very great harm would be wrought to the fortunes of our said gentlemen and citizens, as every member of this Council, in his prudence, very well understands. For the aforesaid dresses which have been cut short would be thrown away, and it would be necessary to make new dresses, which would lead

---

[32] This lament is constant in sumptuary legislation of the sixteenth, seventeenth, and eighteenth centuries. The amount of sumptuary legislation passed at Venice was enormous. For a description of the collections of such laws, see Critical Note 1. For a general survey of Venetian sumptuary legislation, see Giulio Bistort, *Il magistrato alle pompe nella repubblica di Venezia studio storico*, in *Miscellanea di Storia Veneta edita per cura della R. Deputazione Veneta di Storia patria*, series III, t. V. (Venice: Emiliana, 1912).

[33] May 2, 1299, Great Council, A.S.V., *Fractus,* fol. 94.

to great expense. Further, it is convenient that what the aforesaid women have once desired, with the same they should be obliged to be content.[34]

A report by an English ambassador at the beginning of the seventeenth century suggests that the passion for luxury intensified as trade declined: [35]

They here change theyr manners, they have growne factious, vindicative, loose, and unthriftie. Theyr former course of life was marchandising; which is now quite left and they looke to landward[,] buieng house and lands, furnishing themselfs with coch and horses, and giving themselfs the good time with more shew and gallantrie than was wont, and in effect theyr studie is *spantalonirsi* where as theyr old manners would promise more assured continuance[.] After the old manner theyr wont was to send theyr sonnes upon galies into the Levant to accustume them to navigation and to trade. They now send them to travaile [travel] and to learne more of the gentleman than the marchant.

Where the preambles to medieval sumptuary laws suggest concern about luxurious living both because it offended God and consumed wealth, the laws of the last three centuries of the Republic (and they were much more numerous) speak principally about the destruction of private fortunes. The consumption of family wealth was dangerous partly because it might lead to oligarchical power for those who kept their fortunes, and partly because less wealth meant smaller tax revenues,[36] but principally because it so impoverished men that they and their descendants could not afford to serve in the most important public offices. Innumerable seventeenth- and eighteenth-century sumptuary laws speak of the wasteful living of many citizens, the destruction of entire fortunes, and then the inability of these citizens and their descendants to serve the government.[37]

[34] I have used the translation to be found in the essay of Margaret Newett, " The sumptuary laws of Venice in the fourteenth and fifteenth centuries," *Historical Essays by Members of the Owens College Manchester* (London: Longmans, 1902), pp. 247-48. The source is A.S.V., Sen. terra. reg. XV, fol. 38. I am indebted to this article for the preceding remarks on sumptuary laws.

[35] Report of Dudley Carleton, probably of the year 1612, cited by Cozzi, *Il doge Nicolò Contarini,* p. 15n.

[36] Report of magistrato alle pompe, Sept. 16, 1676, A.S.V., Comp. leggi, b. 305, p. 808; and decree of Feb. 20, 1651, A.S.V., Prov. sopra pompe, b. 21.

[37] See April 2, 1644, A.S.V., Senato terra, CXIV, p. 49; and (Senate) Mar. 6, 1732 and Apr. 30, 1781, A.S.V., Prov. sopra pompe, b. 8.

Were as many fortunes ruined through spendthrift living as the preambles to the sumptuary laws imply? Undoubtedly these laws exaggerate. But many contemporary accounts by Venetians, by foreign ambassadors, and by travellers, leave little doubt that huge sums were spent on villas, on clothing, on musical entertainments, and on staffs of gondoliers and servants.[38] Most families lived on fixed incomes from lands and government bonds, and it is natural to surmise that, like their noble contemporaries in France, England, and elsewhere, they often lived beyond their incomes.

Rodolfo Gallo has shown how a wealthy branch of the Pisani family managed to dissipate much of its fortune during the eighteenth century. Almorò Pisani died in 1682 leaving his possessions under a fideicommissum. Under this form of will, his heirs in all succeeding generations were forbidden to part with any of the " immovable goods"—principally lands and buildings— which they inherited. The aim was to force his heirs to be content with their large fixed incomes and not to kill the goose which supplied their golden ducats. But the fideicommissum could not and did not prevent his heirs from selling lands received as dowries or legacies from wives and mothers, nor from selling jewelry and other valuables. Not every generation that followed Almorò was wasteful; there seems to have been the usual sequence of a spendthrift father followed by a thrifty son. But Almorò's grandson used up all his unencumbered possessions to enlarge the family's Venetian palace and to build a magnificent villa on the Brenta River between Padua and Venice.[39] Almorò's great-great-grandson, Alvise, was decidedly a prodigal spender. In order to buy splendid furnishings, to build granaries on his land, and to entertain the visiting king of Sweden, he borrowed heavily on the lands that he could not sell. He served on two very expensive ambassadorial missions in Madrid and Paris and lived for a long time on an expensive scale in London. His financial position became ever worse; his letters to his Venetian agent are marked by bitterness over his situation and a feeling

[38] See Pompeo Molmenti, *La Storia di Venezia, nella vita privata dalle origini alla caduta della repubblica* (7th ed., 3 vols.; Bergamo: Istituto italiano d'arti grafiche, 1927), III, Chap. XI, " La famiglia."

[39] The former is now a handsome conservatory; the latter, a museum at Strà.

that there was no way out. He instructed his agent to sell his family jewels, and he tried to free his possessions from the fidei-commissum. Despite the seriousness of his plight, however, while at Madrid he purchased nine splendid horses, claiming they were a bargain, although he already owned nine horses and three mules. When he left Madrid for his new embassy in Paris—which he had almost refused because of his finances—he sold his table silver; the plan was to buy new silver in Paris, which he did, but it was far more expensive than he had anticipated. His brother, Francesco, feared an inundation of creditors and that Alvise would ruin the family, but he could do almost nothing to restrain him from his extravagant spending. After the fall of the Republic, the family was forced to sell the villa at Strà (to Napoleon), numerous works of art, their library, a numismatic collection, and part of the Venetian palace.[40]

The problem of the possible decline of noble families' incomes involves two economic and financial topics which Venetian historians have studied very little. These are the rise in prices which took place in the sixteenth and following centuries, and the economic fortunes of those who had lent money to the Venetian government. Recent studies of the way prices rose in areas near Venice indicate that a fairly sharp rise began about 1560. Probably this upward trend was most pronounced in the latter sixteenth century and more gradual thereafter. Then, at the end of the seventeenth century and in the early eighteenth, the Venetian lira declined so greatly in value that the government had to devalue its money by twenty-five percent. This devaluation must have had an effect similar to that of the price rise. One can only speculate about what happened to the incomes of noble families when their money declined in value. If the sixteenth century price rise had the same effect in Venice that it had in other parts of Europe, it struck most severely at industrialists, merchants, and financiers. Landowners probably emerged in better financial condition. The seigneurial class seems to have fared very well in such areas as Spain, Sicily, Naples, and Lombardy. Many Vene-

---

[40] Rodolfo Gallo, "Una famiglia patrizia; I Pisani ed i palazzi di S. Stefano e di Strà," *Archivio Veneto*, XXXIV-XXXV (1944), pp. 65-228, esp. pp. 185-201.

tian nobles had, by the latter sixteenth century, bought land, and these men may even have benefitted from the rise in prices.[41]

Many nobles, however, received large revenues from the interest paid on their shares in the public debt, and these men may have suffered greatly from the rise in prices and also from the way the government handled the repayment of money it had borrowed. Probably it would be impossible to discover to what extent the noblemen who lent money to the government in the various military crises of the last three centuries were dependent on the interest paid by the government on these debts. According to Gian Francesco Priuli, who in 1574 proposed liquidating the various debts, there were " many [nobles and cittadini] who receive four, six, and even ten and more thousand ducats of interest a year from the Mint. . . ." The opposition of some of these creditors to Priuli's liquidation proposal suggests that they depended heavily on the generous rate of tax-free interest. As the interest on the various loans in these centuries often was paid for many decades before liquidation was possible, the rise in prices, as well as the devaluation of the currency, must have cut into many incomes. To make matters worse, the government was obliged, on at least two occasions in the seventeenth and eighteenth centuries, to reduce the interest it paid on some loans; undoubtedly some families suffered from the resulting reduction in their incomes. But eighteenth century discussions of the wealth or poverty of the nobility make no mention of this problem. A very serious blow to the government's creditors came only with the fall of the Republic in 1797. The " democratic " government installed under Napoleon's auspices refused to assume responsibility for the debts of the former aristocratic republic; the Austrians who next ruled Venice followed this example; and Napoleon in 1806 allowed only a partial liquidation of the republican government's debts. Antonio Lorenzo da Ponte wrote in 1801 that " thousands, and thousands of Investors . . . lost

---

[41] On the price rise in Venice and its effects elsewhere see Fernand Braudel, " La vita economica di Venezia nel secolo XVI " (*La civiltà veneziana del rinascimento,* Venice: Centro di cultura e civiltà della fondazione Giorgio Cini, 1958, pp. 81-102), pp. 90-95 and Braudel, *La Méditerranée,* pp. 402-408. On the reduction of the value of the lira see Luigi Einaudi, " L'economia pubblica veneziana dal 1736 al 1755 " (*La Riforma Sociale,* XIV, 1904) p. 186.

in the fall of the Venetian Aristocratic Government either all of their wealth or an important part of it. . . ." The loss of income after the fall of the Republic, however, is not relevant to this study.[42]

Economic opportunities for nobles had decreased and the impulse to waste fortunes seems to have grown stronger. It remains now to examine the evidence which indicates that the nobility did in fact become poorer during the last three centuries. There are, to begin with, scattered bits of evidence that show how groups of nobles lost their wealth because of unfavorable economic situations or suggest that the proportion of poorer nobles was increasing. The preamble to a law of 1625 indicates that the decline of trade had by then begun to reduce the number of men who could afford to serve in expensive posts: " Because of changes in the times and in commerce over a long period of years no one seeks election to several of the Governorships and offices. . . ." [43] It was also during the early decades of the seventeenth century that the poor nobles seem first to have been numerous enough to become a strong political force. The spirited Renier Zen led them at this time in attacks on the wealthy patricians and the privileges which these *grandi* accorded each other. The group which backed Zen made up little less than two-thirds of the Great Council.[44] This number, however, must have included not only poor nobles but many of moderate means who merely wished to see justice done.

Whatever the proportion of poor nobles may have been, it

[42] On the debt reduction in the 1570's see Ugo Corti, "La francazione del debito pubblico della repubblica di Venezia proposta da Gian Francesco Priuli," (*Nuovo Archivio Veneto*, VII, 1894), pp. 331-64, and Daniele Beltrami, "Un ricordo del Priuli intorno al problema dell'ammortimento dei depositi in zecca, del 1574," in *Studi in onore di Armando Sapori* (Milan: Cisalpino, 2 vol., 1957), II, pp. 1071-87. For the reductions of interest paid on the public debt in the eighteenth century see A. Vietti, *Il debito pubblico nelle provincie che hanno formato il primo regno d'Italia* (Milan: Quadrio, 1884), pp. 126-28; Lorenzo Antonio da Ponte, *Osservazioni sopra li depositi nella Veneta zecca* (Venice, 1801), p. 25; and Einaudi, " L'economia pubblica," p. 187. For the nonpayment of the Republic's debts after its fall, and possible effects on the nobility see Vietti, *Il debito pubblico,* pp. 9-10; Filippo Nani Mocenigo, *Del dominio Napoleonico a Venezia (1806-1814) (note ed appunti)* (Venice: Merlo, 1896), pp. 66-67; and da Ponte, *Osservazioni,* p. 3.

[43] Apr. 1, 1625, A.S.V., Av. del comun, 34/16, fol. 23v.

[44] Cozzi, *Nicolò Contarini,* p. 247.

increased during the exhausting War of Crete which Venice
fought against the Turks from 1646 to 1669. Thirty Venetian
noble families comprising about one hundred adult males returned from the island colony to the mother city. According to
a Venetian observer, those who returned were in a state of " desperate poverty "; one of the returning nobles candidly described
them as " miserable relics." [45]

There seems to be equally positive evidence of an increase in
the number of poor nobles in the amounts that were granted
each year to some of them as pensions—or doles. These pensions
have nothing in common with the pensions that were given during this period in some European courts to wealthy and influential noblemen. They were distinctly intended to help families who
were in serious straits. Most of them went not to noblemen themselves but to orphaned spinsters. As there were occasional accusations of fraud regarding these pensions, the figures should be
viewed with just a touch of skepticism. Unfortunately, there are
no figures on the actual number of pensions (except in 1791) or
their average size—there are only yearly records of the total
amounts of ducats allotted. These totals indicate a striking increase in the amount paid to noble families.[46]

[45] The former writer was the author of the *Relazione della Serenissima*. He says
(p. 27) that those who returned from Crete numbered 200. The other source is
Giannantonio Muazzo, *Del Governo Antico,* fol. 60. Muazzo, who came from Crete,
says there were 30 families including 100 adult male members.

[46] The amount for pensions in 1670 is to be found in A.S.V., Senato rettori, filza
77, report of *deputati ed aggiunti alla povvision del danaro pubblico,* Jan. 10, 1670,
inserted to accompany decree of Feb. 18, 1670, which is lacking. For the amount
of 1679, see " Bilancio delle Entrate Pubbliche," MS, Correr, Cic. 2251, fol. 375v.
As separate sums went to pensioners of the secretary class and on the mainland, it
seems fairly certain that the amounts I have given above were for pensions to nobles
only. Apparently pensions were given to the same categories as those listed in eighteenth-century balances, which are explicit as to who were recipients. The totals
for 1736-55 can be found in *Bilanci generali della repubblica di Venezia* (3 vols.;
Venice: R. Commissione per la Pubblicazione dei documenti finanziari della repubblica di Venezia, 1903), III, p. 106. (Publication was later continued by the R.
Accademia nazionale dei lincei.) The source used by the editors was A.S.V., Dep.
ed agg. etc., pp. 330-76 (the annual balances), which provided my totals for 1760-
1780. The totals for 1785 and 1790 are from Dep. ed agg. etc., reg. 270 and 275.

1670	29,621	1760	93,039
1679	29,188	1765	81,706
1736	39,542	1770	88,285
1740	44,989	1775	102,604
1745	43,997	1780	114,298
1750	57,018	1785	121,752
1755	59,707	1790	130,179

While the sums paid out in pensions quadrupled, the number of the nobility was decreasing by about thirty percent. In 1791 about 1,100 noble persons—men, women, and children—were receiving pensions.[47]

There is other evidence of the decline of wealth in the difficulty which the Republic experienced in finding men who could accept offices which required considerable personal wealth. The preamble of the law of 1625—already quoted—related this lack of men to the decline in trade. This law was followed by other similar ones. In 1749 a law passed by the Senate attributed the same lack of potential office-holders to " the doldrums into which the private economy of the families has fallen." [48] There were " few—very few " families who could accept expensive offices, a nobleman remarked twenty-five years later in the Great Council; and during the eighteenth century a large number of formerly wealthy families declined to the point where they were dependent on the minor lucrative offices for their livelihoods.[49]

It goes without saying that the ideal way to discover whether the nobility became poorer during the last three centuries of the Republic would be to compare the incomes of members of the nobility in different periods. Unfortunately, the Venetian records of tax returns are not up to the task. They are too sporadic, are based only on income from " immovable goods " (houses and

[47] A.S.V., Camerlenghi di comun, reg. 13 and 14, *Indice provvigionati nobili* (1791). The declining value of money probably contributed only slightly to the rise in the totals of the pensions granted. The official devaluation of Venetian coinage by twenty-five percent took place very early in the eighteenth century.

[48] Apr. 26, 1749, Senate, A.S.V., Prov. sopra pompe, p. 21.

[49] Nicolò Balbi, *Relazione delle cose occorse in Maggior Consiglio nella correzione dell'anno MDCCLXXV e delle dispute in esso tenute per nuova aggregazione alla veneta nobiltà estesa in Xci lettere da N.B. P.V.* [Nicolò Balbi, Patrizio Veneto] *Con inserte tutte le Parti proposte Documenti e Carte Nell'Opera stessa citate,* MS, Correr, Cic. 2650, pp. 161-99.

land), and are compiled in a manner that makes them difficult to consult.[50] Price rises in the second half of the sixteenth century, furthermore, would make it very difficult to make a meaningful comparison of the figures for one decade with those of another.

If really specific information about the wealth of the nobility in different centuries is not to be had, some general estimates, made by contemporaries, are available. Most of them are very rough guesses and quite untrustworthy. The famous diarist, Marino Sanuto, for example, wrote in about 1500 that of his 3,000 fellow noblemen the majority lived in serious need; but at another point he remarks that one could buy everything in Venice " because everyone is rich." [51] Of two men writing in about 1680, one says that many nobles are " exceedingly wealthy "; the other says that " there are more than a Hundred, but not a great number, in the Roll of the Wealthy. . . ." [52] Such statements obviously are not very useful.

But some of the estimates by contemporaries seem to deserve more respect. In 1423, Doge Tomaso Mocenigo made a speech in which he attempted, unsuccessfully as it turned out, to dissuade the nobility from electing Francesco Foscari as his successor after his death. Foscari, he said, would wreck the flourishing Venetian economy with an aggressive foreign policy, and Mocenigo proceeded to describe the wealth of Venice in boastful but fairly accurate terms.[53] Of interest here is his claim that there were in his time 1,000 noblemen who had incomes of 700 to 4,000 ducats a year. Apparently men with incomes in this range were at least comfortably off. Three and a half centuries later,

[50] See Bernardo Canal, " Il collegio, l'ufficio e l'archivio dei Dieci Savi alle Decime in Rialto," *Archivio Veneto,* XVI (1908), pp. 115-50, 279-310.

[51] The first remark is to be found in Gino Luzzatto, *Storia economica dell'età moderna e contemporanea* (4th ed.; Padua: Cedam, 1955), pt. I, p. 83. The second is from Sanuto's *Cronachetta,* pp. 48-49.

[52] *Esame Istorico Politico,* p. 49 and *Relazione della Serenissima,* p. 46.

[53] One version of Mocenigo's speech—the best, according to the editors—is published in *Bilanci generali,* Vol. II. doc. 81. The original is in Marc., It. VII, 794. The same version is published, with discussion, in Heinrich Kretschmayr, *Geschichte von Venedig* (3 vols.; I-II, Gotha: Perthes, 1905-1920; III, Stuttgart: Perthes, 1934), II, pp. 617-19. On the fairly high reliability of this statistic, see Luzzatto, " Sull'attendibilità di alcune statistiche economiche medievali," *Studi di storia economica veneziana,* pp. 280-82.

in an official report made in 1784, Andrea Tron cited these statistics in a way which implied that in his time there was far from
this number of nobles with comfortable incomes.[54] A contemporary of Tron wrote that of 1,200 noblemen then living, a tenth
were " opulent," 300 were in reasonably easy circumstances, and
the rest were more or less in need, with many in extreme want.[55]
This would give a total of about 420 men with incomes that contemporaries considered adequate—a large drop from the 1,000 of
whom Mocenigo boasted. As we shall see, the total number
of nobles was also declining, but not as fast as the proportion
of wealthy men.

In a study of the " city of the lagoon " perhaps the most tell-
ing statistic of all is that, whereas the noble families had at one
time employed 3,000 gondoliers, in the last years of the Republic they had in their service less than 300.[56]

There was still, of course, a considerable number of very
wealthy nobles in Venice at the end of the eighteenth century.
Wealthy families as they died out bequeathed their possessions
to related wealthy families.[57] Other families continued to build
or to maintain large incomes through trade within the Venetian
possessions,[58] careful management of their estates, " good " marriages, and so on. Thus " the rich get richer. . . ." Still it seems
fair to conclude from all the evidence discussed that between the
sixteenth and eighteenth centuries the number of nobles who
were wealthy by Venetian standards sharply decreased.

---

[54] Romanin, *Storia documentata*, IX, 103. Tron did not make a comparison of
incomes in his time with those of the earlier period, apparently because he believed
that in Mocenigo's time the ducat had had ten times its eighteenth-century value.
[55] Leopoldo Curti, *Memorie istoriche e politiche sopra la Repubblica di Venezia,
scritte l'anno 1792 da Leopoldo Curti* (Venice: Parolaris, 1812), pt. II, p. 1n. See
Critical Note 3 for a discussion of Curti.
[56] Molmenti, *Storia di Venezia*, III, p. 332n.
[57] Balbi, *Relazione delle cose*, pp. 228-30.
[58] An example is the Sagredo family which did very well in the seventeenth century by trading in timber from Friuli. (*Esame Istorico Politico*, p. 20).

CHAPTER III

THE NOBILITY DECREASES IN NUMBER

At the same time that wealthy Venetian noblemen were becoming ever fewer, there was an impressive decline in the total
number of noblemen. During two centuries and a half their
number declined markedly from decade to decade. If the ghost
of Andrea Gritti, the famous doge who had presided over the
Great Council when the nobility was most numerous, had returned in 1797, he would have been astonished to see how few
men there were to attend meetings in the once packed council
hall. This demographic change, I should mention here, involved
not only the nobility but the upper middle class of Venice as
well.[1] Here, however, I will be concerned only with the decline
in the number of noblemen, as it was they who ran the Venetian state.

In contrast to the question of the wealth of the nobility, the
decline in the total number of noblemen can be shown with
some precision. The data for the sixteenth century are somewhat difficult to interpret, but after 1594 there are lists of noblemen that seem to be based on scrupulously-kept records and that
make it quite easy to keep track of the number of men over
twenty-five (i.e., of age to hold public offices).[2]

The number of noblemen seems to have increased steadily
between the middle of the fifteenth and the middle of the sixteenth centuries. It was because of rising numbers that it was

[1] Information on the changing proportions of the Venetian nobility (men, women, and children) and cittadini in the total population of Venice can be found
in Beltrami, *Storia della popolazione,* pp. 71-77. In contrast to Beltrami, I am concerned in this chapter only with the decline in the number of men over 25, since
it was they who were eligible for public offices. This decline has been studied very
superficially and ineptly in "Una delle cause della caduta della repubblica veneta." (See Preface, footnote 1.)

[2] See Critical Note 2 for the sources and my use of them.

necessary in 1460 to add a third urn to the two in the Great Council from which noblemen drew the lots which entitled them to nominate candidates for office.[3] From a remark made by the diarist Marino Sanuto, it appears that in 1493 there were about 2,420 noblemen who were entitled to hold offices; twenty years later the number was up to about 2,570.[4] The preambles to laws indicate that the number continued to rise during the 1520's. The text of a law passed at the beginning of that decade begins: " The number of noblemen having greatly increased. . . ." And in 1527 the body of nobles was described as " molto augmentata." [5] From a list in Sanuto's diary it appears that in the latter year there were about 2,620.[6] Meanwhile the census figures for the city's total population indicate a rise from an estimated 115,000 in 1509 to 168,627 in 1563. The upward trend may have held true at least this late in the century for the nobility as well, because records show that there was a steady rise in the number of births of nobles between 1530 and 1569, while the number of deaths remained constant.[7] On the other hand it appears from a list of noblemen in 1550 that their number had decreased somewhat to about 2,520.[8] There is a good deal of room for error in all of these figures but this much appears sure: In the first two-thirds of the sixteenth century the nobility numbered at least 2,500.

Two things could halt this increase: a decline in the number of children born or a decided rise in the number of deaths. As it happened, the latter occurred first, with war and plague taking a tremendous toll in the 1570's. Francesco da Molin wrote of the " many contagious illnesses of an evil quality [which] prevailed throughout Italy " in 1570,[9] and it must have been one of these which accounted for the unusual number of deaths of

[3] Sandi, *Principi di storia civile,* pt. II, II, p. 700. Sandi attributes the addition of a third urn to the rise of the number of nobles and cites " Lib. C. Avog."
[4] Sanuto, *Cronachetta,* pp. 221-22. Marc., It. VII, 90 (8029), pp. 349-50.
[5] Apr. 15, 1520, Great Council, A.S.V., Comp. leggi, b. 241, no. 337; July 31, 1527, Great Council, *loc. cit.,* b. 199, no. 351.
[6] *Diarii,* XLV, cols. 569-72.
[7] For the population figures, see Beltrami, *Storia della popolazione,* p. 59. For birth and death data see Table 10 of the appendix of his book. His figures on births from 1530 to 1664 apparently come from Marc., It. VII, 173 (8160) and the numbers of deaths in the sixteenth century from Marc., It. VII, 353 (7931).
[8] See Critical Note 2.
[9] Molin, *Compendio,* p. 15.

noblemen in that year—a figure two and a half times the annual rate in the previous decade.[10] Only a year later, twenty-nine noblemen were killed fighting the Turks in the glorious but costly naval battle of Lepanto.[11] Then the horrendous plague of 1575-77 caused a staggering loss of life. The total population of Venice dropped from about 170,000 to 120,000 in two years.[12] The nobility fared somewhat better than the general population, since they were better fed and could desert the city for havens on the mainland.[13] A commission of doctors from Padua reported that those who were struck by the plague were principally "poor people, tired and nourished without any discretion."[14] But if the poor were the worst sufferers, this was little consolation to the families of about 300 noblemen who died of the *peste* in 1575 and 1576.[15] According to the contemporary historian Morosini, "many of senatorial rank also perished, and sometimes one who had declaimed in the morning in the *Collegio* was lacking in the evening," seized by the plague.[16] The men aged twenty-five or more had previously numbered about 2,500: How many were there after the 1570's? There are no accurate sources for the number of adult noblemen just before and after this decade, but to judge by two census figures, the number of noblemen was cut by a quarter[17] to a figure of about 1,875.

The nobility made a good start toward recovering in the next few decades. By 1594, there were about 1,970 noblemen aged twenty-five and over; fifteen years later there were about 2,090.[18]

[10] Beltrami, *Storia della popolazione,* Table 10. There were 180 deaths in 1570, as compared to an annual average of about 69 in the 1560's.

[11] Romanin, *Storia documentata,* VI, p. 314.

[12] Beltrami, *Storia della popolazione,* p. 57.

[13] Molin, *Compendio,* p. 70. He says the typical attendance at Great Council meetings was down from 1,500 to 250-300.

[14] Their report is in Marc., It. VII, 806 (9557).

[15] Correr, Grad. 43, pp. 286-91, lists 318 who died during the last half of 1575 and in 1576. Presumably not all died of plague. I believe the figures derive from those of the *magistrato alla sanità* and refer only to men aged twenty-five or over.

[16] Romanin, *Storia documentata,* VI, 350.

[17] According to these two censuses there were 2,435 noblemen aged 18 or more residing in Venice in 1563, and 1,821 in 1581. (Correr, Donà 53, and Marc., It. VII, 2469 [10583], pp. 209-23.)

[18] Correr, Donà 225, and Correr, P.D. 368b. The sources for these and subsequent years give quite accurate figures on the number of noblemen. See Critical Note 2.

This figure for 1609 is the highest recorded point which the nobility reached in its recovery from the losses of the 1570's. It represents a gain of about 200. There is some reason to think that many noble families had made a conscious effort to make up for the loss of so many of their members. The fact that there were more births in the 1580's, when the nobility had been terribly decimated, than in the 1560's, suggests this.[19] Perhaps the partial recovery was the aftereffect of a high mortality of the old and sick during the plague; this might have resulted in a lower death rate among the nobility in the immediately following decades. One student of the plague of the 1570's maintains that it struck young and old alike,[20] but the plague of the 1630's (see below) seems to have killed more of the older than the younger men.

The recovery was sharply halted by this second plague, which struck Venice in 1630 and 1631. The nobility fell in numbers from 2,000 in 1620 to 1,660 at the end of 1631.[21] But this time, in contrast to the period after the plague of the 1570's, there was no impressive recovery in the succeeding decades.

Even before the second of these plagues, the nobility had begun to shrink slightly in numbers. This process continued through the seventeenth century and accelerated in the eighteenth. As with all demographic changes, the causes are no doubt extremely complex. The rest of this chapter is devoted largely to discussion of possible reasons for the diminution. These are offered more as suggestions than as positive and final explanations.

A German biologist, Ernst Rodenwaldt, has studied the causes of the decline in size of the Venetian nobility.[22] What he did essentially was to compile and analyze statistics on all marriages and births of the members of twenty-one families which he considered " qualitatively representative " of the nobility, dur-

---

[19] Beltrami, *Storia della popolazione,* Table 10.

[20] Ernst Rodenwalt, " Pest in Venedig, 1575-1577. Ein Beitrag zur Frage der Infektikette bei den Pestepidemien West-Europas," *Sitsungsberichte der Heidelberger Akademie der Wissenschaften, Mathematische-naturwissenschaftliche Klasse,* 2. Abhandlung (1952), 179.

[21] Correr, Cic. 37 and 18. Two hundred and seventeen " nobili e patrizi " died of the *peste* according to *Cenni storici sopra la peste di Venezia del 1630-31.* . . . (Venice: Graziosi, 1830), pp. 8-9. The author is listed as " C^{re}.F."

[22] " Untersuchungen." Full citation in preface, footnote 1.

TABLE 1

Population Changes [23]

Ven. Noblemen		Pop. of Venice		Percentage of Noblemen in		Mainland Pop.	
Year	Total	Year	Total	Population [24]		Year	Total
		1509	(115,000)	1509	2.2 pct.		
1513	(2,570)						
1550	(2,520)					1548	1,438,741
		1552	158,069	1552	1.6 pct.		
		1570	(170,000)				
		(*PLAGUE TOOK PLACE*		*1575 - 1577*)			
		1581	134,871	1581	1.4 pct.		
1594	1,970						
1620	2,000						
		1624	141,625	1624	1.4 pct.		
		(*PLAGUE TOOK PLACE*		*1630 - 1631*)			
1631	1,6660						
		1633	102,243	1633	1.6 pct.		
1645	(1,620)						
(127 FAMILIES ADDED)		1696	138,067				
1719	1,710						
1775	1,300						
(TEN FAMILIES ADDED)							
1797	1,090	1797	137,240	1797	.8 pct.	1790	2,225,335

ing the sixteenth, seventeenth, and eighteenth centuries. Fortunately for such a study, the " Golden Books " of births and marriages [25] contain most of the accurate information Rodenwalt needed, while genealogies, kept by the patrician Marco Barbaro

[23] Sources for the number of Venetian noblemen are indicated in the footnotes of surrounding pages and in Critical Note 2. The information in columns 2 and 4 of the table comes from Beltrami, *Storia della popolazione*, pp. 59, 69-70, 72. Figures in parentheses are estimates.

[24] These are approximate percentages based on the data in columns 1 and 2.

[25] After 1506 the Avogaria del Comun kept careful records of births of noblemen, and after 1526 it kept records of their marriages. These are the well-known " Golden Books."

and others during the three centuries, supply dates of death and other useful supplementary material.[26]

From Rodenwaldt's tables, it is clear that the decline in the number of nobles did not result from a lack of fertility—in either of the senses in which that word is used by demographers. There was no decline in the physical ability to have children, nor in the actual production of children per family. Rodenwaldt studied the number of children produced by marriages over the sixteenth, seventeenth, and eighteenth centuries. He excluded from consideration childless marriages, since in these cases a different factor (discussed below) might be at work. Counting the children of all other marriages, he found that in each century there were about the same number of children: an average of 5.7, then 5.6, and then 5.8.[27] These figures indicate no decline in the ability to have children. I believe they also show that the nobles were not trying to limit the number of children in their families. If there had been any attempt to limit family size, we might expect to find a development comparable to that Louis Henry has shown for Geneva, where upper middle class families clearly practiced birth limitation after about 1650. Before that date only about 15 or 20 percent of the families Henry studied had three to five children; most had considerably more. After about 1700 over 50 percent of the Genevan families had three to five children.[28] Turning to Venice, we find that the families Rodenwaldt studied, counting childless marriages, averaged in the three centuries 4.29 children, then 4.0, and then 4.46.[29] Family size was thus fairly constant and it appears unlikely that the Venetian nobility began to practice family limitation during this period.

Analyzing the number of marriages which produced no children or only one child, Rodenwaldt discovered something he con-

[26] One set of the *Arbori di patrizi veneti,* commonly known as *Il Barbaro,* is in the Archivio di Stato di Venezia. The Correr library also has a set: Cic. 2498-2504. On these, see Critical Note 1.

[27] "Untersuchungen," p. 16, Table 2.

[28] Louis Henry (*Anciennes familles genevoises: Étude démographique: XVIᵉ-XXᵉ siècle,* Institut national d'études démographiques, Travaux et Documents, Cahier n° 26, Presses universitaires de France, 1956, Chap. IV).

[29] "Untersuchungen," Table 1. I have adjusted the figure of 4.97 supplied by Rodenwaldt for the eighteenth century to allow for the fact that some eighteenth century marriages are not reported in the genealogies he used. I assumed that, as in the preceding centuries, about twenty-five percent of the marriages were childless.

siders significant in accounting for the decline in the number of nobles. In the sixteenth and seventeenth centuries there was a high number of such marriages, as this table[30] indicates:

TABLE 2

PROPORTION OF CHILDLESS AND "ONE-CHILD" MARRIAGES (VENICE)

Century	Childless Marriages	Marriages With One Child	Together
16th	24.9 pct.	18.2 pct.	43.1 pct.
17th	24.0 pct.	16.0 pct.	40.0 pct.

There can be little doubt that these proportions are high. The incidence of sterility (i.e., inability to have a child or another child) for Genevan couples in the same period was as follows:

TABLE 3

INCIDENCE OF STERILITY (GENEVA)

Age of Wife	Percentage Sterile
20	3
25	8
30	13
35	21
40	39

There are similar figures for England in the nineteenth century.[31] Rodenwaldt's explanation of the high figures hinges on the large proportion of marriages which produced only one child. He considers these particularly significant. " It is one of the most widely known and the surest facts of epidemiology," he says, " that in a population where there is a high percentage of marriages which produce only one child, gonorrhea is widespread." As a result of the infection transmitted to the mothers at the

[30] *Ibid.*, p. 16, Table 2. Rodenwalt could not get reliable data for the eighteenth century.
[31] Henry gives the figures for Geneva and England in *Anciennes familles*, p. 126. According to Isidor Clinton Rubin, M.D. (" Sterility," *Encyclopaedia Britannica* [Chicago-London-Toronto, 1957], XXI, pp. 398-99), 85 percent of married couples have children.

conception of the first child, further conceptions after the birth of this child become impossible. To Rodenwalt, it appears fairly certain that this disease must have been prevalent in the nobility and that it was responsible for the high number of single births. According to him, it also explains the unusually high percentage of childless marriages, since the same disease which made women barren would have rendered many men sterile.[32] An objection to this explanation for the diminution of the nobility is that their number increased and the annual number of births rose during much of the sixteenth century, even though the percentage of childless and " one-child " marriages was actually a little higher during this period than it was in the following century when the numbers of the nobility declined rapidly. During the sixteenth century, obviously, gonorrhea—if it was indeed prevalent—was not enough by itself to cut down the size of the nobility. At best, it can have operated then and later only as a contributing factor. But to give Rodenwaldt his due, he attributes equal importance, as will be shown below, to some attitudes and customs of the nobility.[33]

There are other possible explanations of the high proportion of marriages which produced no children or only one child. One is that families may have been purposely limiting births. But I have already explained my doubts that Venetian families limited births even in the eighteenth century, and the practice certainly would not account for the high figures for the sixteenth century, when birth limitation was little practiced in Europe. In any case, it is particularly unlikely that families would limit their size so drastically. Another explanation for the childless and one-child marriages may be that nobles were marrying at a late age when they were approaching sterility. There are no statistics for the ages at marriage in Venice, but it is possible that men did marry late, especially after the custom of restricted marriages (discussed below) was adopted in the late sixteenth or seventeenth centuries. But this explanation would seem not to apply to most of the sixteenth century. Also, while the men may have

---

[32] " Untersuchungen," p. 24. According to Lenz, " 'One-child sterility' is quite typical of gonorrhea." (Erwin Bauer, Eugen Fisches, Fritz Lenz, *Menschliche Erblehre und Rassenhygiene,* 3rd ed., 2 vols., [Munich: Lehmans, 1936], vol. 2, p. 54.)

[33] See " Untersuchungen," p. 24, for his general conclusions.

married when middle-aged, it is far from certain that they would have chosen middle-aged brides. Thus it is not as if both partners in many marriages would have been approaching sterility. To me, the most plausible explanation for the high figures for marriages which produced no children or only one child is simply that the genealogies and birth records Rodenwaldt used are not accurate. It may be that the births of many children who died in infancy were never recorded. This is a common problem with the sources for demographic studies of the early modern period. Meanwhile, it seems relevant to the general question of childlessness to mention that in 1760 a Venetian gazette carried an advertisement by a "Gypsy Astrologer" named Domenico Bernardi announcing to "Families of importance, which are threatened with lack of offspring," that he had a secret method " ensuring that within the space of a year. . . ."[34]

The most important cause of the demographic decline was a social one. When it was proposed in 1684 to create new noble families to raise war revenues and compensate for the decline in numbers,[35] Michele Foscarini told the Great Council that the decline resulted from the custom of restricted marriages.[36] He was referring to the practice of many nobles families, even those with numerous sons and daughters, of having only one or two of these children marry. As the Barbaro genealogies show, sometimes the oldest brother, just as often a younger one, was the only male member of the family to marry. Other brothers remained bachelors or entered the Church, while of the daughters

---

[34] Gasparo Gozzi, Gazzetta veneta, (Bruno Romani, ed., 2 vols., Milan: Bompiani, 1943), I, p. 44.

[35] Rodenwalt ("Untersuchungen," pp. 22-23) is mistaken in believing that the nobility only recognized in the later eighteenth century the shrinking of their numbers, its causes, and its potential harmful effects. See Chapters IV and V regarding the discussion in the seventeenth century of the need to ennoble new families. Muazzo (Del Governo Antico, fol. 69v) in the seventeenth century tabulated past attendance figures of the Great Council, and discussed reasons for the diminution.

[36] Degl'istorici delle cose veneziane, I quali hanno scritto per Pubblico Decreto (an edition of official Venetian histories), Pietro Garzoni, Istoria della repubblica di Venezia (2 Vols.; Venice: Manfrè, 1719-20), I, pp. 94-95. Garzoni reports a paraphrase of Foscarini's speech. The mention of single marriages is not to be found in Foscarini's own report of his speech (see below). But whether he said it or not, its inclusion in the contemporary work of Garzoni indicates that the nobles of his time were aware of this cause of the decline.

one, or at most two, married and the others remained at home or entered convents.

It is impossible to be precise about when this custom, found also in other parts of Europe,[37] began in Venice. Because the Barbaro genealogies do not always note men's marriages if these resulted in no children, it is often difficult to identify the generation that initiated the custom of restricted marriages. Most noble families evidently adopted the practice after 1450 and before 1650. Perhaps in the majority of these families it was the generation that reached maturity about 1550 that first chose to have only one brother take a wife. The astute nobleman, Giannantonio Muazzo, who in about 1670 became interested in the diminution of the nobility, came to this conclusion.[38]

One asks himself how a family could decide which brother should marry. For, as remarked above, it was not always the oldest who took a wife. Frequently this member of the family devoted his career to government service and chose to remain single, the better to devote all his efforts to the state. In a considerable number of cases it was the youngest son who married. See p. 68 This may have resulted from a habit of delaying any marriage until all were of age, by which time it may have appeared wisest to let the most vigorous marry in the interests of preserving the family line. In any case, the traditional unity of the Venetian noble families goes a long way toward explaining how it was possible for a group of brothers to come to the necessary agreement. As was explained in Chapter I, a rather extraordinary sense of unity and co-ordination of its efforts marked the family as an economic, a political, and a social unit. How this could encourage an agreement that only one brother should marry is suggested by the wish expressed in a testament of Stefano Tie-

---

[37] In Lombardy, for example, Beccaria lectured in 1769 on the dangers to the public economy of too few marriages. See *Scrittori classici italiani di economia pubblica* (50 vols., Milan: Destefanis, 1803-16), Vols. 18-19, *Elementi di economia pubblica di Cesare Beccaria milanese,* part I, chap. III. Louis Henry (*Anciennes familles,* pp. 51-54) shows that in Geneva the proportion of unmarried men and women increased greatly from about 1550 to about 1750 and then declined rather slowly over the next 100 years.

[38] Muazzo, *Del Governo Antico,* fol. 70.

polo in 1550 "that all the [five] said sons of mine should live together at equal expense nor may they divide nor separate the goods and their persons until the last of the above named sons . . . shall have completed thirty years of age. Praying them, and pledging them [*astrenzendoli*] by the passion of our lord Jesus Christ to love one another and to have regard for the ages of each other. Doing this they will do a thing pleasing to our lord God and to their Honor."[39] The requirement that all live together until the youngest of five sons had reached the age of thirty would tend to limit marriages. Certainly it suggests a belief that not all would marry.[40] Presumably there is a limit everywhere to the number of women who can live in harmony under one roof.

When only one of several brothers married, it was probably inevitable that there be suspicions and accusations of immorality. Some contemporaries—French for the most part—wrote that the woman whom one brother had married often served as wife to all.[41] If true, this form of polyandry is at least an extraordinary demonstration of the sense of unity of the noble families.

In the sixteenth century, a branch of the Tron family provides an illustration of the extent to which restricted marriages were a conscious matter, designed to guarantee survival of the family without, it appears, letting it become too large. Paolo Tron had six sons, as this excerpt from the family tree[42] shows:

[39] A.S.V., Testamenti notarili, 1229, no. 125, fols. 105v-106v. These pleas to children to remain under one roof can be found in medieval Venetian wills.

[40] Three of the sons eventually married, but the second did so only when the first son's marriage proved unfruitful; and the third, when the second had provided no heir. (A.S.V., Barbaro, VII, p. 84). Thus the custom of restricted marriages was in effect, as it had been in the preceding generation.

[41] Molmenti (*Storia di Venezia*, III, p. 332) cites six persons who claimed that this custom did prevail to some extent and quotes a quatrain in Venetian dialect about it. Molmenti believes that the writers "generalized from some rare case of turpitude."

[42] A.S.V., Il Barbaro, VII, p. 142.

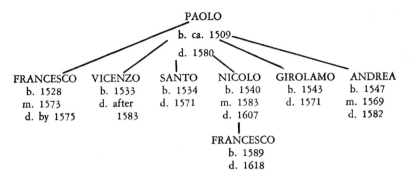

PAOLO
b. ca. 1509
d. 1580

FRANCESCO	VICENZO	SANTO	NICOLO	GIROLAMO	ANDREA
b. 1528	b. 1533	b. 1534	b. 1540	b. 1543	b. 1547
m. 1573	d. after	d. 1571	m. 1583	d. 1571	m. 1569
d. by 1575	1583		d. 1607		d. 1582

FRANCESCO
b. 1589
d. 1618

His youngest son, Andrea, was the first to marry. Four years later Andrea had had no children, and there may have been reason to fear that he would have none in the future. (As we shall see, this is suggested by the father's will.) Two other brothers, furthermore, had died (probably at the naval battle of Lepanto) in 1571. The family's chances of survival must have seemed a little tenuous. Now the oldest brother, Francesco, married at the age of forty-five. It would seem that he married only in order to insure continuance of the family line. But Francesco himself died sometime in the next couple of years; and when the father, Paolo, wrote his will in 1575, he was genuinely concerned lest the family die out. Only three of his six sons were now alive, and Andrea still had no children. "I want to urge strongly," he said, "that if Andrea should have no children, his other [two] brothers should not let our family die out, there not being any others but them." [43] Nicolò and Vicenzo waited, however, and only when Andrea died in 1582 did they make their decision. Nicolò married the following year at the age of forty-three. Six years later he had a son, Francesco, whose appearance saved the family from extinction.

One element behind the nobles' adoption of a custom which limited the size of their families may have been the love of luxurious living which had become so strong during the Renaissance and certainly persisted throughout the eighteenth century. Michele Foscarini, in his speech in the Great Council, blamed the habit of single marriages on "our customs" which, he said,

[43] A.S.V., Testamenti notarili, 1265, XV, p. 40.

were "corrupted by idleness and luxury; which persuade us to forego having heirs, rather than leave them unable to meet the various expenses." [44] The result of this determination to maintain a high standard of living is evident in a Longhi painting of a wealthy branch of the Pisani family. Four handsomely-dressed, middle-aged eighteenth-century gentlemen stand behind one seated woman with four children. Three of the four had apparently been elected to preserve the family fortune; one, to preserve the family.[45]

Shrinking family incomes were another reason to avoid large, spread-out families of several branches which would dissipate the common fortune. Muazzo affirms that the custom of only one of a group of brothers marrying was introduced in the latter half of the sixteenth century as a means of keeping a family rich even when its income had declined. After Western nations had cut into Venetian commerce with the East, he said, the nobility saw that it was difficult to become rich in trade and turned to landholding on the Venetian mainland. Even though land provided a fairly sure income, the returns were smaller than those provided by trade. Unable to increase their wealth, the families elected to decrease their size.[46] It is interesting that they chose to effect this by permitting only a few to marry and have children, rather than by allowing many to marry and then aiming at very small families. Rodenwaldt's tables indicate that the average noble family included over four children.

An economic factor also prevented the marriages of many girls whose fathers could not or would not provide large dowries. An interesting example was a niece of Andrea Soranzo. In his will of 1571, this nobleman left a sufficient sum of money to pay her entrance and keep in a convent. But he also stipulated that a specified larger sum should be given her as a dowry "when it pleases God that the Strength [wealth] of the family improving it reaches a point that she might marry." [47] Family pride

[44] Degl'istorici, Michele Foscarini, Historia della repubblica veneta (Venice Louisa, 1720), p. 161. Foscarini published his own speech in his history of Venice late in the seventeenth century.
[45] The portrait is reproduced in the illustration section of this book.
[46] Muazzo, Del Governo, fol. 70.
[47] A.S.V., Testamenti notarili, 1249, t. II. fol. 169.

occasionally worsened the financial problem since it was necessary to fix a sufficiently large dowry to enable the daughter to
marry not any noble but one " of our condition." [48] One haughty
Corner girl refused a Sagredo who was willing to marry her for
a comparatively modest dowry. The proud noblewoman chose to
become a nun instead. (Another sister, previously destined to
the convent, cheerfully accepted the spurned man.) [49] Many a
noble daughter, no doubt, entered a convent so that her family
might save a dowry. Nonmarriage of noble girls, however, was
not such an important cause of the decline of the nobility as was
nonmarriage of the men. For a child to enter the Venetian
nobility it was necessary only that the father be a noble; the
mother could be an approved member of the middle class. It is
unlikely that many noble men failed to marry because of the
number of girls who had entered convents.

An increasing number of young noblemen during these centuries entered the Church. The number of patricians wearing
some form of religious garb doubled between 1620 and 1760.[50]
Religious devotion may have played a part in this development,
but probably more important was the desire to avoid marriages
and conserve family fortunes. The tendency to enter the Church
must have hastened the extinction of many a small family. Presumably the day had passed when the last survivor of a family
could or would imitate the actions of a twelfth-century Venetian
noble monk whose family had almost disappeared. According to
legend he left his monastery, married a doge's daughter, fathered
seven sons and thus insured continuance of his family, and then
returned to the cloister.[51]

[48] Girolamo Grimani used this phrase in 1569 in establishing dowries of 10,000
ducats for each of his daughters. (A.S.V., Testamenti notarili, p. 12, no. 116.)
[49] When an old, nonnoble friend ventured to congratulate the Corners, they told
him to save his congratulations for the Sagredos, to whom they had condescended
to give a daughter. Distinzioni Segrete, pp. 10-11.
[50] The following are the numbers of noble ecclesiastics at different times during
the seventeenth and eighteenth centuries:

       1615-20 ca. . . . . .   83 (Correr, Cor. 6)
       1635-38 ca. . . . . .   87 (Correr, Cor. 12)
       1706 ca.   . . . . . 123 (Correr, Cor. 95)
       1760   . . . . . 166 (Protogiornale per l'anno MDCCLX . . .)

[51] Andrea da Mosto, I dogi di Venezia con particolare riguardo alle loro tombe
Venice: Ongania, n.d.), p. 266.

In addition to the desire for luxury and display and the declining revenues, it may be that the popularity of the fideicommissum tended to cut down the size of many families. This system for bequeathing one's possessions had its roots in Roman law but had taken on new significance in medieval times as a means of maintaining the power and fame of a family by conserving wealth and decreeing a fixed line of succession. For this study it is important to note these principal characteristics of the fideicommissum;

1. It was composed of "immovable goods"—principally land.
2. These goods could not be sold or in any way alienated by an heir.
3. This property was indivisible. That is, it had to go to only one heir.
4. The possessions had to be inherited according to an order of succession which was established by the testator. Usually he required that they go to first-born sons in perpetuity.

The fideicommissum seems to have appeared in Italy for the first time in the eleventh century but only gradually acquired all of these characteristics. In any case, it became widely diffused in Italy only in the sixteenth and seventeenth centuries in imitation of the custom of the Spanish conquerors. It then became exceedingly popular with the upper class and even with many peasants. The fideicommissum acted to cut down the size of families, of course, since only the eldest son inherited the family wealth and was in a position to marry. He was often obliged to see to the needs of his brothers and sometimes to provide dowries for his sisters. Younger brothers usually remained bachelors and often became ecclesiastics; many young women entered convents.[52]

There is probably a good deal of truth behind the remark by Muratori in the eighteenth century that "not rarely everything is in Fideicommissum. . . . And this Fideicommissum limited to a single person, and only in the male line; nor is there anything left for the brothers, nor is there anything with which to marry

_On p. 63_
"It is said
That the
youngest
son was
frequently
The only one
to marry"

[52] For this summary and for the references to Muratori and Filangieri, I am indebted to Biagio Brugi, " Fedecommesso (Diritto romano, intermedio, odierno)," Il digesto italiano: Enciclopedia metodica e alfabetica di legislazione, dottrina e giurisprudenza (Torino: Unione tipografico-editrice, 1884-1921), XI, pt. I, pp 588-660. See also Antonio Pertile, Storia del diritto italiano, (2nd ed., 6 vols. Turin: Unione tipografico-editrice), IV, pp. 148-55.

off the daughters, the sisters, the cousins, etc." [53] With great bitterness the Neapolitan legal writer, Gaetano Filangieri, explained in the late eighteenth century how the fideicommissum reduced the number of landowners and, in consequence, the population. " A father who can afford to have only one of his sons rich, wants to have only one son. In the others he sees just so many dead weights for his family. The degree of unhappiness in a family is computed by the number of sons. . . . So many younger sons deprived of property, and consequently of the right to marry, oblige as many girls to remain single. Deprived of husbands, under pressure from their fathers, these unfortunate creatures are often obliged to shut themselves up in cloisters, where with their bodies they bury forever their posterity." [54]

In Venice the fideicommissum was rare in the Middle Ages. This might have been expected from the fact that comparatively little wealth was in the form of land; it was desirable, moreover, to keep that small amount available for conversion into capital and not tie it up by provisions of a fideicommissum. In the sixteenth century and afterward this form of entail became much more common in Venice.[55] Many men began writing wills which forbade their beneficiaries to sell the goods they inherited. In contrast to the practice elsewhere, however, they left their possessions to *all of their sons,* not just the oldest.

The adoption of the fideicommissum is partly explained by the fact that this kind of will was already popular elsewhere in Italy as a result of Spanish influence. But it was probably even more the decline of trade and the unpromising economic picture which caused nobles to adopt this device for ensuring that the wealth earned in good times should remain in the hands of their heirs. One noble explained in 1596 that he was inaugurating a fideicommissum " because I want [my possessions] to remain perpet-

---

[53] Ludovico Antonio Muratori, *Dei difetti della giurisprudenza* (2nd ed.: Venice: Pasqualy, 1743), p. 186.

[54] Gaetano Filangieri, *La scienza della legislazione,* (6 vols.; Venice: Santini, 1822), I, bk. II, p. 201.

[55] I have found innumerable wills in the period 1550-1600 which institute fideicommissa. See A.S.V., Testamenti notarili: 1172, fol. 244 and fol. 244v; 1249, t. I, fol. 145; 1249, t. II. fol. 166. A law of May 21, 1617 (Great Council) says that there had been numerous legal contests " da certo tempo in qua " in connection with wills involving the fideicommissum. (A.S.V., *Arcangelus,* 9v.)

ually in our Family, because I wish that the hard work done by our ancestors, with so much sweat, should not go for naught." [56] Then there was the important fact that wealth now consisted chiefly of land, which was the traditional basis of this kind of will. The fideicommissum, finally, appeared to be the perfect means of maintaining the wealth necessary for the honor of the family, and for combating possible spendthrift tendencies in any heirs. In 1605 Nicolò Tron wrote a will establishing a fideicommissum which stipulated that his lands could be alienated only by an heir who was a regular member of the Senate. His remarks are a fine expression of the desires and fears that might motivate the use of this kind of will: "And this I have ordered because I desire and wish that my possessions remain with the male members of my line for their honor and so that they may never be in need and may occupy public offices with dignity, hoping that those who are admitted to the government of this State will not be so insane that they will want to sell what belongs to them and their sons in order to waste it. . . ." [57] So this legal advice served the same purpose that was accomplished by having only one son in a family marry; it prevented the dispersion of the family's wealth.

One might question whether the fideicommissum and the custom of restricted marriages were merely two parallel means used to conserve wealth or whether using this type of will actually led to or encouraged the tendency toward single marriages. Elsewhere it made single marriages obligatory, according to Filangieri, because all of the possessions went to a single son who alone could afford to take a wife. But the great difference between the fideicommissum generally and the institution as it was found in Venice is that in the Republic possessions were rarely left exclusively to the eldest son. At most, various land holdings might be left to him to provide an income to finance a political career; or he might have special rights over the family palace.[58]

[56] A.S.V., Testamenti notarili, 1172, fol. 244v. Will of Domenico Contarini.
[57] A.S.V., Testamenti notarili, 1249, t. II, fol. 46v-47.
[58] For an example, see the will of Giustiniano Contarini (died 1567), who left his residence in fideicommissum to his older son, Giorgio, to be followed by Giorgio's eldest son; he wanted his other possessions to be divided equally among his sons. (A.S.V., Testamenti notarili, 1262, t. I, fol. 73v.)

In most wills, possessions were left to all sons equally.[59] When they reached manhood, they were free to divide the possessions. But since they usually remained under the same roof, and since the fideicommissum prevented them from alienating any of the "immovable possessions," and since unmarried brothers usually left their possessions to the children of the brother who had married, estates usually remained intact. So there was no need for a custom of primogeniture. It would have been a betrayal of the Venetian tradition of co-ordination of efforts within the family. Therefore, if the fideicommissum cut down the number of marriages in a given family, it was not because it put all the wealth in the hands of the oldest brother. This is proven by the fact that frequently it was a younger brother who married.

If this kind of will restricted marriages at all, it was probably rather by making the family's wealth less flexible. Incomes had already been reduced when they came to be based not on trade but on land rents. The fideicommissum would have made it more difficult to obtain through the sale of land the large amounts of money which were necessary for the enormous costs of weddings, for the construction of the new palace which might be necessary if more than one brother married, or for all the necessities of a family. It would also have made it more difficult to raise the money for a dowry, although some wills made provisions for the alienation of lands for dowries.

There is very little direct evidence that the fideicommissum actually had the effect of restricting the number of marriages. But in 1775, a nobleman who was discussing in the Great Council the small number of marriages of noblemen, did name, among such other causes as high dowries, concern with self instead of family and fatherland, and unequal distribution of wealth, "the too strong chain of the perpetual and unlimited fideicommissa." [60]

The reasons for the custom of restricted marriages probably included in some measure all those discussed—love of luxury, declining and inflexible incomes, the attraction of Church careers

---

[59] For a rare exception see the will of the very wealthy Doge Marino Grimani, who in 1605 stipulated that his possessions be inherited by eldest sons who, however, had to give 500 ducats yearly to their brothers. (A.S.V., Testamenti notarili, 1249, t. I, fols. 181-82.)

[60] Balbi, *Relazione delle cose,* p. 248.

—and perhaps others as well. Whatever the causes may have been, Venetian nobles married less and less. One of Rodenwaldt's tables shows this tendency.[61]

TABLE 4

PERCENTAGE OF THOSE WHO MARRIED AND THOSE
WHO REMAINED SINGLE

Century	Men Who Reached Marriageable Age	Married	Single
16th	2,274	49.0	51.0
17th	1,542	40.0	60.0
18th	795	34.0	66.0

What is even more surprising than the restricting of marriages is that in some families no one married. Rodenwaldt shows how this happened in families where there was only one son to carry on the line.[62]

TABLE 5

MARRIAGES OF ONLY SONS

Century	Only Sons Who Married	Only Sons Not Married
16th	140 (82.0 pct.)	31 (18.0 pct.)
17th	98 (65.3 pct.)	52 (34.7 pct.)
18th	24 (35.3 pct.)	44 (64.7 pct.)

There was also a steadily increasing number of families with as many as five or six male heirs, none of whom married.[63] It seems extraordinary that these proud and ancient families should have been willing to see their very names disappear from the rolls of the Venetian nobility.

The preceding pages have dealt with a number of possible reasons for the decline in the number of births, of which the

[61] "Untersuchungen," Table 6, p. 19. The article does not make it perfectly clear that in this table he took into consideration only those men who reached marriageable age, but in response to a letter I wrote to him, Dr. Rodenwaldt kindly reassured me on this point.
[62] "Untersuchungen," Table 6, p. 19.
[63] Ibid., Table 5, p. 18.

foremost was the restricting of marriages. The number of births dropped off decade by decade after the 1580's. Where approximately 1,200 children had been born to noble families in that decade, the number was lower by 100 in the 1590's, lower by another 100 in the 1600's, and continued to decline.[64] For this reason, while the general population of Venice rose considerably in the decades after the plague of the early 1630's, the nobility maintained a steady decline. Although more than a hundred families were added to the nobility between 1646 and 1718, they did little more than compensate for the constant attrition, since the nobility numbered only 1,710 men at the end of that period. During the eighteenth century the nobility accelerated the rate of its suicidal course. In 1775, when the nobility decided to accept more families, there were only 1,300 men. When the Republic fell in 1797, the Great Council included only 1,090 noblemen.[65] Between the middle of the sixteenth century and the end of the eighteenth, the number of noblemen had diminished by more than fifty-five percent.

The decline in numbers of the Venetian nobility adds a new dimension to the economic decline discussed in the preceding chapter. Dwindling economic opportunities and a new tendency to dissipate wealth in luxurious living were probably not the only factors which reduced the number of men who had enough wealth and talent to be effective in the government. The decrease in the size of the nobility and the dying-out of many families also reduced the number of wealthy men. Foscarini implied in the speech discussed earlier that it was particularly in the most outstanding families that single marriages were the custom. Whatever the number of wealthy men may have been in the middle of the sixteenth century, that number must have declined considerably while the nobility as a whole diminished by fifty-five percent during the following two and a half centuries. Naturally the wealth of a rich family which died out would not dis-

---

[64] The figures for annual births in Beltrami's *Storia della popolazione* (Appendix, Table 10) may be somewhat unreliable. After 1600 Beltrami offers two sets of figures for each year (from different sources) and these differ by as much as 50 or 100 for each decade. The general downward trend is clear, however, in both sets of figures.

[65] *Protogiornale per l'anno* . . . [1775-1797] . . . *Ad uso della Serenissima Città di Venezia* (Venice: Bettinelli, 1775 and 1797).

appear, but it is unlikely that it went to poorer nobles and enabled them to enter the ranks of the wealthy. The richer families were likely to be related to other families in comfortable circumstances. Consequently the wealth of a family that had died out would probably go to other related wealthy families, or to churches, monasteries, and the like.

Over a period of two and a half centuries the Venetian nobility diminished by more than half, and there was a noticeable decline in the number of men with the wealth necessary to make them effective members of a ruling class. These changes, the next chapter will show, caused serious difficulty in finding men to rule the state. This problem might never have arisen if it had been possible for able and wealthy men to enter and be assimilated in the nobility. But from the fourteenth century to the middle of the seventeenth, the nobility was restricted to the same group of families and, when new families were subsequently ennobled, the method used was poor and inadequate. The changes that took place in the nobility between about 1575 and the fall of the Republic were great, but it is not really surprising that changes of some kind took place. To put a class label on a particular group of families and expect this group to maintain the same character over several centuries was like trying to carry water in a sieve.

CHAPTER IV

A MANPOWER SHORTAGE IN THE GOVERNMENT

During the first half of the seventeenth century the Venetian
ruling class began to feel the effect of what might somewhat
anachronistically be called a manpower shortage. This happened
because, while the number of principal government offices remained approximately the same, the number of noblemen who
were willing, qualified, and able to serve had begun to decrease
sharply. During the seventeenth and eighteenth centuries it
became harder and harder to find men who could and would
serve in the important posts: in governorships and embassies, in
the busy administrative and financial committees of the Senate,
and as *savi grandi*, ducal councilors, and members of the Council of Ten. This lack of qualified candidates for principal offices
seems to have been one of the most serious aspects of the Venetian period of " decadence."

The lack of qualified candidates for the principal offices may
have first become a matter of public concern during the 1630's.
According to the author of a little treatise on the Venetian nobility written during the latter seventeenth century, there was
danger during the 1630's and the early 1640's (before a large
number of new families were ennobled) of having to give even
the most important offices to those who did not merit them. This
writer implies that the danger arose from the decline in the number of nobles, because he says that there was talk of recalling the
Venetian noble families living on Crete or of granting Venetian
nobility to aristocratic families living on the mainland.[1] Giannantonio Muazzo, a well-informed Venetian nobleman who wrote at

[1] *Della nobiltà, trascorso istorico, al Re Cristianiss. Luigi XIIII*, MS, A.S.V.,
Comp. leggi. b. 294, fols. 800-812. The anonymous author, probably French rather
than Venetian, says that he based his essay on published sources.

75

about the same time, says that "from about 1630 after the Plague, there was talk of increasing [the nobility] in some proper and decorous manner. . . ." [2]

The shortage of able officeholders apparently was first discussed in the Great Council in 1645 when the War of Crete, fought against the Turks between that year and 1669, had just broken out. The *Collegio* proposed to sell the privileges of Venetian nobility to five families with the aim principally of building up a war chest and incidentally of compensating for the loss of the noble families which had died out. In defending the proposal, Giacomo Marcello told the Great Council that "the foundations of the government have been the number of Patricians and their unity, and our State cannot stand on few and weak supports. The [government] offices require the minds and hearts of many; and how can one select the best man, if there are few candidates from which to choose?—the selection will be a forced not a free one. Those marks of honor—the offices of the Republic—should be not so much birthrights as rewards for ability." [3] His remarks and the preamble to the bill to accept new families make it clear that the lack of men for offices was then a well-recognized problem.

Forty years later, the shortage of men in the ruling class seems to have been considered even more serious. At least there is far more anxiety in the remarks made by Michele Foscarini in 1684 when he persuaded the Great Council to revive the sale of rights to nobility. Sad as the rapid disappearance of many noble families was, he said, "It is even more painful to consider that the distribution of offices in this Great Council may one day become completely odious; that there may be more offices than subjects; that it may not be possible to reject the poor candidates and reward the good ones; that the men who can undertake the more demanding posts of the Republic may disappear and those who replace them will not have the means to do so [properly] . . . we should not deceive ourselves; we see the beginnings already; the competition for the offices is so rare that these . . . seem to me to be almost abhorred, and men work out expedients so that

---

[2] *Del Governo Antico*, fol. 70.

[3] *Degl'istorici*, Battista Nani, *Historia della repubblica veneta* (2 Vols.; Venice: Louisa, 1720), p. 90.

they will not be elected. But the mutual need which one citizen has of his fellow is the bond which holds our society together. If this bond should loosen, those customs will change which until now have preserved an internal peace and allowed our Republic to endure longer than any other."[4]

Lack of public spirit is often the cause of difficulty in finding men for public offices, and this may indeed have been one of the reasons for the problem in Venice. There are some indications that there was increasing political apathy in the ruling class, and it is easy to find plausible explanations for this apathy. One might be the proportional increase in the number of poorer nobles. The attention of these men was no doubt concentrated mainly on earning a living in the mediocre offices which were designed chiefly as sinecures. They would not have been interested in holding the most important posts which were not paid at all or frequently involved expenses exceeding the salaries. Poorer men would also have known that, even if they were ambitious, their lack of wealth would prevent them from reaching the more important offices because they could not afford these posts and because lack of wealth meant lack of the requisite prestige. A lack of wealth also meant that they could not afford a good education, and without such an education they would doubtless lack both the ability and the interest to take an active part in the government. In the early seventeenth century Venice established an Academy of Nobles where a small number of sons of poor nobles were educated at public expense. But one patrician observed that " when he has finished five years [there] a Student has not learned the Latin language well, and he has picked up little more than reading and writing."[5]

The decline of commerce may have convinced many of the more influential families that they no longer had an important stake in Venetian affairs. Senate memberships ceased to offer these families opportunities to vote for their interests—and incidentally those of the state—in such matters as galley voyages, the regulation of state banks, and the public debt; it no longer

[4] Foscarini, *Historia*, p. 161.
[5] *Relazione della Serenissima,* p. 115. According to Curti (*Memorie istoriche,* p. 70) the education provided in his time (1792) was satisfactory, but limited to a small number of boys.

provided a listening post where they could learn about political developments with interesting financial implications. Many others may have lost interest in the government as Venice fell into the ranks of lesser political powers in the years after the Italian wars of the early sixteenth century. In the East, Venice fought one debilitating war after another against the Turks; toward the West she maintained continual neutrality. According to the patrician historian Marin who wrote just after the fall of the Republic, the War of Morea, fought against the Turks at the start of the eighteenth century, resulted in a disillusionment that caused many even of the more conscientious nobles to lose interest in the government.[6]

And then there were many pleasant distractions in seventeenth- and eighteenth-century Venice. This was the great period of cafés, gambling, pre-Lenten celebrations that lasted for months, the comedies of Goldoni, private concerts and operas, the scholarly or convivial " academies," and especially the easy, gay life in estates on the mainland. The banks of the Brenta and Terraglio rivers were lined with handsome classical and baroque villas in which the wealthier families held their almost unending house-parties.[7] The attractions of this easy life in the country were often stronger than the feeling of duty to the state; more than once the Senate had to send out general invitations to the negligent to return to duty. " For the grave needs of the Republic," one of these began, " the zeal and love of its citizens is needed, both with unceasing attendance in the Offices and Councils and with the use of hard work and their wealth in the important external Posts. . . . The Senate . . . should not relax its efforts at all because of the changing of the season since the dangerous circumstances of the Country are not changing. . . ." All were asked " to remain in this area in the present autumn season." These reminders were sent out from time to time.[8]

---

[6] Carlo Antonio Marin, *Storia civile e politica Del Commercio de' Veneziani* (8 vols.; Venice: Coleti, 1798-1808), VIII, p. 313.

[7] For a most interesting picture of all the activities, intellectual and otherwise, of the nobility in the last two centuries, see Molmenti, *Storia di Venezia*, III, Chaps. 3 and 10.

[8] Sept. 29, 1704, Senate, Comp. leggi, b. 348, p. 372. Enrico Besta, *Il senato veneziano. Origini, attribuzioni, e riti* (Miscellanea, Series II, Vol. V; Venice: Deputazione (R.) veneta di Storia Patria, 1899), p. 282, quotes a slightly altered

Just before the overthrow of the Republic, a Venetian nobleman, with democratic leanings and a grudge against the government, penned a sketch of the meetings of the Senate which is
certainly amusing and quite possibly accurate. He said that most
of the sessions consisted of a string of decrees which were read
with incredible speed and listened to very little or not at all by
the senators. These men spent the time strolling, or chatting
about trifles, including their amours; in winter they stayed by the
fire in a room next to the Senate hall. After the readings, all the
decrees were voted on together and the session adjourned. When
this happened quickly, all the senators were jubilant because they
were relieved of the annoyance of what they called a " long *Pregadi*" (Senate session). They used to exult: " Short *Pregadi*,
short *Pregadi!*, " happy because they could return so much the
sooner to their pleasures.[9]

Probably then, considerable political apathy did develop during the long Venetian decline, but there is little clear evidence
of it. Most of those who wrote about the patricians' lack of
interest in their government did so in the latter eighteenth century. Recent studies, furthermore, have shown that even in the
last two centuries of the declining Republic there were always at
least a few men in the government who took a keen interest in
affairs and were willing to sacrifice their time and wealth in filling important offices.[10]

It seems to have been primarily the changes in the nobility dis-

---

version of the same deliberation, and says similar ones were passed on Oct. 22,
1715 and Sept. 28, 1745. I have not found either of these in Senato terra or the
deliberations of the Great Council.

[9] For a description of Giovanni Pindemonte, the writer of this description of the
Senate, see below in this chapter and Critical Note 3. The description comes from
an untitled treatise on the decadence of the Venetian government which Pindemonte wrote in 1796. (Giovanni Pindemonte, *Poesie e lettere di Giovanni Pindemonte*, G. Biadego [ed.] [Bologna: Zanichelli, 1883], p. 344.)

[10] In addition to the already-mentioned biographies of Nicolò Contarini by Cozzi
and Leonardo Donà by Seneca, see Nerina Conigliani, *Giovanni Sagredo* (Venice:
Emiliana, 1934); Giovanni Tabacco, *Andrea Tron (1712-1785) e la crisi dell'aristocrazia senatoria a Venezia* (Trieste: Smolars, 1957); Marino Berengo, *La società veneta alla fine del settecento: Ricerche storiche* (Florence: Sansoni, 1956);
Massimo Petrocchi, *Il tramonto della Repubblica di Venezia e l'assolutismo illuminato*, in *Misc. di Studi e Memorie* (Dep. di Storia Patria per le Venezie) (Venice: Ferrari, 1942), VII; and Roberto Cessi, *Storia della repubblica di Venezia* (2
vols.; Milan-Messina: Principato, 1946), II, Chap. VII.

cussed in the preceding chapter, and not political apathy, that created the problem discussed by Marcello and Foscarini in the Great Council. The "manpower shortage" was caused mainly by the decline of the number of nobles and especially the number of wealthy men. No longer was there a great body of men of varying talents and experience and wealth from which to choose 100 or so of the most qualified to fill the important and demanding offices.

What happened to two families, the Basegios and Valiers, makes clear on a small scale how the economic and demographic changes affected the Venetian political scene. The Basegios are probably the best example of men whose poverty excluded them from public offices. Their poverty dated at the latest from the early fourteenth century—long before the decline of Venetian trade—when they are mentioned as one of several poor families that backed Bajamonte Tiepolo in his unsuccessful insurrection.[11] A seventeenth century writer described the Basegios as a family that no longer had any distinction because of their poverty and because there were so few men in the "miserable" branches of the family that still survived.[12] Certainly few and probably no members of the family reached any of the principal offices in the last three centuries of the Republic. A letter to the government from a Venetian town in Istria in 1612 gives an idea of the position to which the Basegios' poverty consigned them. According to the writers, who pleaded with the government to pay the noble governors of their city better, few nobles wanted to serve in Isola because of the very low salary. When they were governed by a gentleman "whose restricted fortunes do not permit a better post," he was often required to remain for a long period until a successor could be found. The noble then serving in Isola was one Giovanni Domenico Basegio.[13]

The branch of the Valier family that produced two doges in the seventeenth century was probably as wealthy as the Basegios

---

[11] The author of a discussion of the nobility in the seventeenth century claims to have read this in a chronicle of the Tiepolo insurrection. (*Distinzioni Segrete*, p. 25.)

[12] *Descrizione delle nobile famiglie venete* . . ., Ms. Correr, Cic. 2166. There is no numeration in this little book, but the families are listed in alphabetical order.

[13] Letter of Aug. 11, 1613, A.S.V., Great Council, filza 25, filed with decree of May 16, 1617.

were poor. It was eventually removed from the political scene, not by poverty, but because the line died out completely. Members of this house had served the government for generations as senators, generals, members of the Council of Ten, and in other posts. Perhaps it was in order to maintain their wealth and position that the family began to restrict marriages during the sixteenth century and subsequently even to limit family size. Massimo Valier, who died in 1573, had four sons; of these, only Silvestro married. Silvestro had only one son, Bertucci, who in turn had one son named Silvestro. In each of these generations the combination of great wealth with ability permitted very useful service to Venice. The earlier Silvestro served on the Council of Ten. His son, Bertucci, was an excellent orator and an able governor and ambassador. His wealth and ability won him the position of doge in 1656. Bertucci's son, Silvestro, may have been less able than his father but he was inspired by the same zeal for public service, which in his will he says he drank with his mother's milk. On special embassies he spent huge sums of money to maintain the Venetian tradition of a public display of magnificence. Eventually he was elected doge, this being the first time a father and son had held the office in many centuries. But Silvestro had no brothers, and when he died this distinguished branch of the Valier family disappeared.[14]

It was the loss, many times multiplied, of families such as the Basegios and Valiers, which caused a lack of nobles capable of holding important offices in the seventeenth and eighteenth centuries. It was a nagging problem, with which the ruling class was slow to come to grips.

Of all the offices in Venice, it was probably the governorships of the subject cities that felt the decline of the ruling class most acutely and obviously. Venice ruled its *Terra Ferma* in northern Italy and Dalmatia by means of noble governors who presided in the cities and outlying forts. The principal cities, such as Bergamo, Brescia, Verona, Vicenza, and Padua, were each ruled by two men. The *podestà* was responsible for judicial and general

---

[14] For the family genealogy and useful information, see the Barbaro genealogies. (Vol. VII, 68v-69v in the Correr copy, MS, Cic. 2504.) For Doge Silvestro Valier's will: Marc., It. VII, 480 (7785), pp. 311-26.. For brief biographical sketches of both doges, see Andrea da Mosto, *I dogi di Venezia*, pp. 247-49, 279-82.

administrative matters; the *capitano* was in charge of the area's
military organization. In the lesser places the two offices were
sometimes combined; sometimes the governor bore another title
such as *conte, castellano,* or *provveditore.* All told, over 100
noblemen occupied these positions. The lesser governorships
paid enough to offer a livelihood to poorer men. But about fifteen of the more important ones, particularly those in the five
cities mentioned above, did not by any means pay enough to meet
the expenses of a governor who wanted to live in the splendor-
ous style befitting Venice.[15] Customs which gained increasing
popularity in the later centuries required him to spend huge
amounts on a magnificent arrival in the city, on splendid furnishings in his residence, and on what might almost be called a
court. Only rich noblemen could afford to accept the posts. But
if the great expenses and the enforced sixteen-month separation
from the brilliant life of Venice were undesirable features of
these governorships, the offices were nevertheless important as
rungs in the ladder of offices leading to the highest, most hon-
ored positions. The richer nobles, furthermore, probably felt a
civic obligation to serve at least occasionally as governors. It
appears that there was no great difficulty in finding men for these
positions before about the middle of the sixteenth century.

As early as 1558, however, the Great Council was encountering
difficulties in finding candidates for these posts. Four electors
were customarily chosen by lot to propose candidates for a governorship. A law passed in 1558 was designed to force these
electors to do their duty. From the wording of the text of the
law it appears that the electors shirked the responsibility of pro-
posing men for these offices because they feared to make enemies of the men they nominated.[16] It is interesting that this difficulty in obtaining candidates for governorships appeared some

[15] The author of the *Relazione della Serenissima* says (p. 14) that in the governorships of Brescia, Bergamo, Verona, Vicenza, Padua, Udine, Chioggia, and some
others of the *Terra Ferma* and Dalmatia, many of which required two men, " the
expense greatly exceeds the salary."
[16] Great Council, *Rocca,* May 15, 1558. Other evidence of a desire to avoid governorships during the sixteenth century could probably be found easily enough. In
1578, for instance, Leonardo Donà was elected *podestà* at Brescia " against my
will." (Seneca, *Leonardo Donà,* p. 118.)

years before the plague of the 1570's and before the decline in
trade which began in the last decade of the century.

There was more than one cause of the difficulties which the
Republic experienced in finding men who were willing and able
to serve as governors. One was the magnificent style of living
which the noblemen felt they had to maintain in these offices.
Wealthy noble governors spent so much on their houses and
public appearances in the subject cities that other nobles could
not meet the standard thus established. At the end of the sixteenth century, fines were introduced for refusals to serve in important governorships;[17] and writing about these seventy-five
years later, Muazzo remarked that " the fine was born after luxury and display made these offices excessively expensive, and consequently difficult and undesirable for many men."[18] During the
seventeenth and eighteenth centuries innumerable laws were
passed decreeing how a governor might live and in what ways
he could spend his money.[19] The preambles to many of them
attribute reluctance to accept election to governorships to the
inability of the noblemen to match the expensive standards
already set.[20]

But inability to match an inflated standard of living was not
the only cause of the lack of potential governors. More basic
than the rise in what had to be spent was the decline in the
number of men who could afford to meet even a simpler standard. When Marcello and Foscarini, whose speeches in the Great
Council are quoted in part above, linked the difficulty in finding
willing candidates for offices to the disappearance of many noble
families, the offices they were thinking of above all were probably the governorships. This seems likely in view of the attention
which the Great Council was constantly forced to pay to election
to these offices. Not only the demographic decline but the economic one as well contributed to the lack of candidates. Pream-

---

[17] Great Council, *Surianus,* Nov. 4, 1599.

[18] Marc., It. VII, 966 (8406), p. 71.

[19] A few laws of this kind were also passed in the sixteenth century, but the bulk
came later. See Bistort, *Magistrato alle pompe,* pp. 277-87.

[20] Among other examples see: Mar. 11, 1653, Senate, A.S.V., Comp. leggi, b. 241,
fol. 647; Sept. 21, 1677, Great Council, A.S.V., Comp. leggi. b. 241, fol. 646;
Apr. 2, 1644, Senate, A.S.V., Prov. sopra pompe, b. 21.

bles to some of the laws dealing with governorships link the
shortage of candidates to the decline of trade. In 1625 it was
noted that "because of changes in the times and in commerce
over a long period of years no one seeks election to several of
the governorships and offices . . ."²¹ And in 1749 the Senate
noted that men were "made incapable [of accepting governor-
ships] by the doldrums into which the private economy of the
families has fallen."²² Luxurious living had also consumed fortunes and thus reduced the number who could serve. One purpose of the general sumptuary laws passed in these centuries was
to preserve family wealth so that there might continue to be
some men who could serve in governorships. The preamble to a
characteristic seventeenth-century sumptuary law says that among
the unfortunate consequences of luxurious living there is, "above
all, that because of the resultant inequality of wealth there is
frequently a lack of subjects who are willing to serve, from
which result the difficulties which are well known. . . ."²³

Men who asked for dispensations from service in governorships to which they had been elected usually pleaded the poor
condition of their family finances. Frequently they pointed out
that other members of their families had previously served in
governorships and that this had consumed much of their wealth.
Pietro Zaguri, to give an example of one who asked for such
a dispensation, begged to be excused from serving as governor
at Rovigo. He had, he said, three paternal aunts, six children,
and five sisters who were in cloisters, all of whom depended on
him for support. A daughter was about to marry, which meant
great expense, and on top of all this, some land which he possessed on the mainland had suffered heavy damage from floods.
He could not assume the post without a "total devastation" of
his fortunes.²⁴ Generally the noblemen who asked for dispensations did not mention what may have been the generic cause of
their inability to serve in the costly governorships, the above-
mentioned "doldrums" of so many family fortunes.

²¹ Apr. 1, 1625, A.S.V., Av. del comun, 34/16, fol. 23v.
²² Apr. 26, 1749, Senate, A.S.V., Prov. sopra pompe, b. 21.
²³ Jan. 5, 1669, Senate (pende), A.S.V., Prov. sopra pompe, b. 21.
²⁴ See A.S.V., Avog. del comun, reg. 616/1, for Zaguri's request for dispensation
and those of many other eighteenth-century noblemen.

The problem of finding men for governorships seems to have become progressively more acute. Laws controlling—or trying to control—expenditures by governors had been few in the sixteenth century, but were passed in profusion during the seventeenth and early eighteenth centuries. Meanwhile the fines for refusals were raised from 500 ducats to 1,000 and then to 3,000; these were in addition to expulsion from the Senate (if the recalcitrant noble belonged to it) and banishment from the city.[25] At the same time, men who consented to serve in some governorships were rewarded with Senate membership.[26] None of these means produced more men of wealth, of course, but they undoubtedly made it easier to persuade or force the available men to accept election to governorships.

One harmful result of the lack of candidates for these posts was that the field of choice was severely restricted. According to the system used in these elections of governors (and some other officers) the Senate met in *scrutinio* and chose one candidate, while four nominators who had been chosen by lot in the Great Council picked four other competitors for the same post. The Great Council then voted on these nominees. According to the nobleman Pindemonte who wrote at the end of the eighteenth century, the Senate's candidate was the only one who was taken seriously; the nominations of the other four were regarded more or less as a joke.[27] This is confirmed by records of the men who competed for offices during the Republic's last two centuries; the Senate's candidate is usually the only one who received a large number of favorable votes.[28] To judge by the ages of men who were elected to the governorships and by the requests for dispensation from these offices, it is fairly clear that the Senate eventually was forced to choose its candidates for a governorship simply by going over lists of men who had reached the minimum age—twenty-five for most of the governorships and thirty

[25] Vettore Sandi, *Principi di storia civile della repubblica di Venezia scritti da Vettor Sandi nobile veneto Dall'anno di N.S. 1700. sino all'anno 1767.* (3 Vols.; Venice: Coleti, 1772), I, pp. 167-68.
[26] See Besta, *Senato,* p. 74; and *Relazione della Serenissima,* p. 111.
[27] See Pindemonte's untitled essay on the decadence of the Venetian government, *Poesie e lettere,* p. 330.
[28] See Marc., It. VII, pp. 813-871 (8892-8950).

for some—and nominating those in the group who had not served before. Among the requests for dispensations are a few from older men who asked to be excused with the promise that their sons would serve as soon as they reached the minimum age.[29] Of course, wealth was also a consideration. Pindemonte claims that the Senate considered only the degree of wealth of possible candidates, not their personal merits. With such a limited field of choice, the election in the Great Council was what Marcello called not " free " but "forced." Presumably he meant that the Great Council was often obliged to elect a man of inferior ability.

The lack of available candidates for the governorships was also harmful because it often meant that it was necessary to administer important cities of the Venetian mainland with one governor instead of the customary two. This had already been the case from time to time in the late seventeenth century, but a special report by the " revisers and regulators of governorships " suggests that it first became an urgent problem in about 1730. A report written by Alvise Foscarini after his return from service as *podestà* at Brescia shows how serious the problem could be. Brescia, he pointed out, was a large and important city, with territory one hundred miles in circumference and a population of several hundred thousand. In such a large area, he said, the responsibilities for military and civil rule—those of the *capitano* and *podestà*—could not be combined in a single office held by one man. Yet before Foscarini and his colleague had taken over their duties there had been but a single governor. This man could not deal with all his duties, and he had been obliged to neglect judicial matters. Only because he had served along with a *capitano*, as the constitution required, had Foscarini been able to dispose of the backlog of neglected cases. When only one man was in charge, Foscarini reported, it was impossible for him to deal with judicial processes, and the result was the " pain and sorrow that arises from nonadministered and longed-for justice." [30]

What has been said regarding governorships is true in many

[29] A.S.V., Avog. del comun. 616/1. For one example, see the letter from Vettor Sandi (the patrician historian of the Venetian constitution) under the year 1754.
[30] Report of May 23, 1745, A.S.V., Misc. cod., 447, no. 35.

respects for posts in embassies. The laws establishing penalties for refusals of governorships apply also to refusals of ambassadorial positions, which suggests a similar increasing reluctance to accept these posts.[31] A seventeenth-century Venetian said of both governorships and embassies that " they are Offices which are ordinarily assigned without any request, because they are considered burdens." [32] A principal reason for the lack of enthusiasm for the ambassadorships was that they were undertaken largely at personal expense, like many similar modern assignments to important capitals. Just as with the governorships, moreover, these posts became ever more costly. Formerly the salaries and expense allowances had sufficed, according to one seventeenth-century French observer, when Venetians had been more frugal. But wealthier ambassadors had wanted to have large staffs of servants, to maintain what were virtually courts, to wear splendid clothes, to gamble, and to enjoy a day-to-day existence as luxurious as that of the princes at whose courts they were temporarily living. Each man, moreover, tried to cut a finer figure than his predecessor.[33]

Most noblemen could not meet these standards. Presumably the difficulty was made much more serious, as it was with the governorships, by the decease in number of the nobility and especially the decrease in the number of wealthy men. Another seventeenth-century French commentator on the Venetian government claims that there were not enough men who could afford ambassadorial posts.[34] But there is less evidence in the form of legislation about the lack of candidates for embassies and the reasons for the lack than there was about governorships. There are no sumptuary laws aimed principally at controlling expenses in embassies, because it was recognized that an ambassador had to spend very heavily; and there is little legislation dealing with election to embassies, probably because these were the affair of the Senate and were handled on a rather personal and informal

[31] Sandi, *Principi di storia civile . . . all'anno 1767,* I, pp. 167-68.
[32] *Esame Istorico Politico,* p. 18.
[33] Casimir Freschot, *Nouvelle relation de la ville et république de Venise* (Utrecht: Poolsum, 1709), p. 264.
[34] Abraham-Nicolas Amelot de la Houssaie, *Histoire du gouvernement de Venise.* [with a] *Supplement . . .* (Paris: Leonard, 1677), p. 194.

basis. Still, penalties for refusals of embassies as well as governorships rose from 500 to 1,000, then to 3,000 ducats. In 1748 it was decided that ambassadors would serve four years instead of three "in order to increase, possibly, the number of subjects who might be elected as Public Representatives." [35]

Another problem which resulted from the changes in the nobility during the "decadent" period concerns the maturity of many men who occupied government positions. The Venetians always had great respect for the wisdom which comes with age. Men were not considered suitable candidates for the dogeship until they were in their late 60's or 70's; in one sixteenth-century election, a 55 year old candidate was considered at a distinct disadvantage because of his youth. Men of 80 could be and were elected to offices, though piteous requests might gain them dispensations. A seventeenth-century writer said that at the bottom of the Golden Staircase in the Doges' Palace there were carved two small piles of fruit covered with straw. These were intended as symbols of the fact that the ambitions of the young had to be preserved until the time when they were mature enough for the various offices in the government. Noblemen were generally chosen for important posts only after they had reached their mid-30's. Minimum ages were not, however, generally stipulated by law; apparently there was no need to formalize what was generally practiced.

In the early seventeenth century it became apparent that the men who were being elected to important offices were frequently too young. This observation recurs frequently in legislation and in the writings of commentators on the Venetian scene. According to an apparently well-informed person who wrote about the Senate in 1675, it had once been customary to choose its members only from among men who had spent about 20 years in lesser posts.[36] Therefore a senator would have been at least 45. Honors at that time, he says, were the "patrimony of the old."

By 1675, however, Senate membership and other honors went

---

[35] Mar. 16, 1748, Great Council, *Bartolinus,* fol. 24. See also the report of the *revisori et regolatori di reggimenti,* submitted Dec. 30, 1748 (Prov. sopra pompe, b. 21) which recommends this change and discusses all sorts of measures to deal with the lack of candidates for governorships and embassies.

[36] *Esame Istorico Politico,* pp. 13-15.

to younger men, with a consequent serious decline in the maturity and experience of the body of senators.[37] As the legislation cited below will show, the situation was already considered serious in 1638; but another anonymous author, writing about 50 years later, looked back to the 1630's as a time when offices were still being given to fairly mature men.[38] From the comparison that he makes between the two periods, it appears that there was a steady trend toward the election of ever younger men to offices.

The most probable explanation for the election of younger men is as follows: The younger men were ambitious for the positions of honor, but, as a discussion below will make clear, they did not care to serve in the intermediate positions which led to the important offices. In earlier years they had been excluded from the latter because there had been an ample number of older men competing against them. But with the decline in the number of nobles, along with their loss of interest in the government and the decrease of their wealth, there were fewer potential office-holders. In these circumstances, it was necessary to " reach deeper into the barrel " and elect younger men. It is no coincidence that laws establishing minimum age limits for several government bodies were passed soon after the plague of 1630-31.

A law of 1639 regarding the judicial councils—the *Quarantie* —confirms the contention that there was a connection between the declining number of nobles and the age problem. This law lowered the minimum age limit of the *Quarantie* from 30 to 28. The somewhat confused preamble to the law begins by recalling that this body had had a minimum age limit of 30 ever since 1334. But now " all is changed." There were not enough competitors for the *Quarantie,* apparently because the minimum age limit for several other offices was also 30. One gathers that the lack of younger men just over 30 resulted from the fact of " this Council [the Great Council] not being as numerous as in past times. . . ." In other words, there were no longer enough men in the group just over 30 years old to spread over the *Quarantie* and the other offices.[39] This law is cited, not to show that

[37] *Ibid.*
[38] Marc., It. VII, 2226 (9205), p. 18.
[39] Jan. 29, 1639, Great Council, A.S.V., *Marcus,* fol. 6v.

immaturity was considered to be a problem in the *Quarantie*, since it obviously was not, but rather to show the connection between the decline in the number of nobles and the necessity which the Great Council experienced of having to elect younger men to important offices.

If immaturity was not considered a problem in the *Quarantie*, it emphatically was so considered in other important posts. Since legislation dealing with the subject had to be approved in the Great Council, where many young men were to be found, it is delicately phrased; but one can easily read between the lines the concern over the immaturity of office-holders. A law of 1634 dealing with offices which gave access to the Senate recalls in its preamble that " our ancestors," in creating the offices of the Republic, had desired to have men with sufficient age—and other requirements—to guarantee effective government. The desire for the posts which gave access to the Senate had, however, greatly declined and now there were few candidates. As what might appear to be an illogical solution to the problem, the Great Council therefore decreed a minimum age limit of 30 for these offices. This, it was evidently felt, would increase the interest of more mature men in applying for these offices which had lost their prestige when they were filled by very young men.[40] The phrasing is tactful, but it is clear that the lawmakers connected the lack of mature candidates for the offices with the fact that younger men had been serving in them. It is unlikely that this new decree could have solved the problem, because there simply were not enough older men available to fill the positions.

Just as for the offices which gave access to it, so for the Senate it soon became necessary to fix a minimum age. The preamble to the law on the subject [41] speaks of three " disorders ": the youthfulness of some senators, frequent refusals of offices (referring perhaps to Senate offices which had lost prestige after the incumbencies of young men), and the fact that the possibility of entering the Senate at an early age encouraged the young men to rush through or avoid serving in subordinate offices which gave access to the Senate.[42] As a result, the law established a

[40] Aug. 27, 1634, Great Council, Comp. leggi. b. 348, fol. 692.

[41] Feb. 20, 1638, Great Council, Comp. leggi, b. 348, fol. 696.

[42] So I understand the phrase "*procurar di passar in breve spatio di tempo dall'uno all'altro magistrato di quelli che entrano nel med^{mo} Cons° de Pregadi.*"

minimum age limit of 35 for the Senate.[43] Two years later, feeling a need to insure experience and maturity in the most important central administrative offices, the Great Council decreed that ducal councilors, members of the Council of Ten, and *savi grandi* be at least 40 years old.[44]

During the seventeenth century the men elected as governors and ambassadors were also felt to be too young. Candidates were generally found for these offices, as was explained above, only with the aid of stern punishments for refusals. It appears that the few volunteers for these posts were ambitious young men who wished to rise quickly to the highest offices and knew that service in the undesired governorships would give them a claim to more desirable posts in Venice after their return from the subject cities. When such men alone volunteered for these offices, the government could hardly turn them down. The author of the *Esame Istorico Politico* comments that:

The Venetian Senate is so courteous in modern times, that in the distribution of Offices, when there is one who asks [for an office], and many who refuse, it finds it easy to satisfy both the former and the latter, without considering whether it might be better to send the man who refuses and hold back the one who requests so that one may use the ability he has acquired and the other, who does not have it, may acquire it.

The result was that there were too many young men serving Venice as governors and ambassadors. The remark quoted was made apropos of Pietro Mocenigo who represented Venice at Rome from 1671 to 1675. This young patrician, after serving only in what was considered an easy post, England,[45] was now in the most difficult and important one. At thirty-nine he was the youngest man who had ever been chosen to represent Venice in Rome.[46] As for the governorships, it has been said already that by the eighteenth century some of these were assigned

[43] Besta says an age limit of 32 had been established in 1431. (*Senato*, p. 81, with footnote.) He cites July 12, 1431, Great Council, *Ursa*, p. 88. But, he says, this was "unobserved" in the early seventeenth century.

[44] Mar. 12, 1640, Great Council, A.S.V., *Marcus*, fols. 25v-26.

[45] Evidently an *ambasciatore straordinario*.

[46] Correr, Grad. 15, *Esame Istorico Politico*, pp. 90-91. It would be almost impossible to check the statement that Mocenigo was the youngest nobleman ever to serve as Venetian ambassador at Rome.

almost automatically to young nobles as soon as they reached the minimum required age.

Yet it might be argued that the lack of men qualified and willing to serve in embassies and governorships and the increasing immaturity of men in a number of important offices would not prove critical so long as there was a nucleus of very able, experienced, public-spirited men to fill the most important offices at the center of the government. As explained in Chapter I, about 100 men were required for this core of the ruling class. Because of their willingness to serve constantly and because they usually moved from one office into another as soon as their terms expired, a number this small sufficed to keep the administration in capable hands. If Venice had continued to produce this class-within-a-class, the Republic might not have suffered too seriously. It is clear from what has been said about the governors and ambassadors that this " ruling nucleus " had in fact declined somewhat, but in those cases special factors—the high expenses of the offices—were at work which might not have reduced the number of men who could serve in some of the other equally important but less expensive posts. So it becomes necessary to make a separate study of the men who could and did serve in other key positions.

Apparently there was never a problem in finding men who were willing to serve as doges, ducal councilors, members of the Council of Ten, *savi grandi*, *avogadori del comun*, and in a few other such posts. Most of these important positions paid salaries and conferred a great deal of prestige and power. In the latter half of the seventeenth century, Muazzo wrote that there were from old times penalties for the refusal of these offices, "yet no one recalls" a refusal.[47] Even at the end of the eighteenth century, when the Great Council decided to ennoble new families so as to have more men to fill offices, one of the "correctors" who spoke in favor of the proposal said that there was no lack of applicants for the posts of "highest honor" but only for the burdensome offices such as governorships.[48]

But while there continued to be men who were willing to

[47] Marc., It. VII, 966 (8406), p. 10.
[48] Nicolò Balbi, *Relazione delle cose*, MS, pp. 214-25.

serve in these offices from time to time for the sake of the honor involved, there was nevertheless a decline in the number of able nobles who year-in, year-out devoted a great deal of their time to these important posts. An examination of the election of *savi grandi,* ducal councilors, and members of the Council of Ten gives an idea of the way the " ruling nucleus " declined and what this decline meant to the government. While not every politically-important nobleman necessarily held one of these three offices during his career, the trend in elections to them is probably fairly typical of what happened with all the leading posts.

In any decade there were 310 elections to these offices. (These comprise ten elections a year to the Council of Ten; twelve elections a year of *savi grandi,* and nine of ducal councilors.) This number of elections did not, of course, mean that 310 different men held these offices, since the most active noblemen were re-elected several times in a decade. The table below shows, for certain decades, how many men held these offices only a few times and how many held them frequently.[49]

TABLE 1

MEN WHO SERVED AS SAVI GRANDI, DUCAL COUNCILORS,
AND MEMBERS OF THE COUNCIL OF TEN

	1560-69	1635-44	1731-40	1780-89
Men who served 1, 2, or 3 times	53	93	123	119
Men who served more than 3 times	35	24	17	23

Assuming that those who held office more than three times (the number being chosen somewhat arbitrarily) were the most able, experienced, and willing men, it appears that there was a decline in the number of such men in the government after the sixteenth century. These figures are small—perhaps too small to

[49] Sources for the names of *savi grandi* were A.S.V., Segretario alle voci, Senate elections, bks. 3, 4, 13-15. 22, 25, 26. For ducal councilors: Segretario alle voci, Great Council elections, III, IV, XIV-XVI, XXV, XXX and XXXI. For the Council of Ten: Marc., It. VII, 825-827 (8904-8906) for the years 1560-1569; A.S.V., Council of Ten, Misc. cod., 62, for the years 1635-1644; A.S.V., Misc., cod. 67 for the years 1731-1740; *Protogiornale per l'anno* . . . [appropriate years] . . . *Ad uso della Serenissima Dominante Città di Venezia* (Venice: Bettinelli), for the years 1760-1789. I took into account only men who were elected for full terms, not those who were elected as replacements for nobles who died or were chosen for other posts.

be statistically meaningful—but the drop from 35 to 24 is impressive. At the same time the number of men who held the key offices only one, two, or three times in a decade more than doubled. The implications of the change become clearer if a comparison is made in terms of elections of experienced and inexperienced men. I drew up the table below from the same data used in Table 1 and based it on the same assumption that men who served four or more times were experienced while the others were not. The table shows how often experienced and inexperienced men were chosen in the 310 elections to these offices which took place in each decade.

TABLE 2

Elections of Experienced and Inexperienced Men as Savi Grandi, Ducal Councilors, and Members of the Council of Ten

	1560-69	1635-44	1731-40	1780-89
Experienced	83 pct.	49 pct.	39 pct.	40 pct.
Inexperienced	17 pct.	51 pct.	61 pct.	60 pct.

In the last centuries, clearly, Venice was more frequently in the hands of inexperienced men.

Why was there a decline in the number of men who continually served in these principal offices? It was partly because of political apathy. Men who cared to serve repeatedly in these posts became hard to find. More important was the general diminution of the nobility and the decrease of the number of wealthy families. The men who served as ducal councilors, *savi grandi,* and members of the Ten had usually been chosen from the wealthier and the politically active families, and these were becoming scarce. From a contemporary treatise on the nobility,[50] we can arrive at a rough idea of the number of these families soon after the middle of the seventeenth century. According to the anonymous author, there were at that time 100 old and rich families. (In referring to families, he probably meant branches of families rather than whole clans such as the Corners, the Contarini, etc). Of these 100, he says, fifty families had members who were active in the Collegio, but among these men there were only about fourteen or fifteen who were capable of being *savi*

[50] *Relazione del anonimo,* in Molmenti, *Curiosità,* p. 425.

grandi, and these men apparently were often given this office. Even this small group seems to have diminished. Over 100 years later, shortly before the fall of the Republic, the nobleman Pindemonte wrote that the *savi* were chosen only from certain of the old and rich families. These families, he says, had greatly declined in number and were in his time "very scarce." (He describes the *savi* from these families as rude, often corrupt, incompetent, and out of contact with affairs.)[51] Pindemonte was wrong in saying the *savi* were chosen only from these families. As the tables above show, the regulars from these families were serving with a rising number of men who held office only one, two, or three times in a decade. I presume these men were elected only because there was no longer a sufficient number of men who could and habitually did serve for repeated terms. Probably they were elected only infrequently because they proved incapable or unpopular, or because they were simply apathetic about holding office.

The same men who served repeatedly as *savi grandi,* ducal councilors, and members of the Council of Ten were likely to provide leading candidates in elections of doges. A study of these elections reveals a decline in the number of candidates which seems to confirm that the inner ruling group was growing smaller. Usually in elections of doges it was apparent to everyone from the start that there were two or three leading candidates. Generally these men were among the nine procurators of St. Mark, men who had been given this honor in reward for long service as ambassadors, supervisors of Venetian armies, admirals, governors of principal cities, and members of the most important administrative councils. It was almost as necessary to be a procurator in order to be *dogabile* as it is necessary now to be a cardinal in order to be *papabile.* It usually happened that on the first ballot by the forty-one electors, none of the two or three leading procurators received the required twenty-five votes. On the second ballot, therefore, another procurator's name was added to the list of those who were voted on, and frequently he too failed to obtain twenty-five favorable votes. The names of other men, usually including all the procurators and some others as

---

[51] Pindemonte, untitled essay on the Venetian government, *Poesie e lettere,* pp 338-39, 348.

well, were voted on in later ballots. Sometimes many ballots were needed before the forty-one could agree on one of the original leading possibilities or some other compromise candidate.

For the sixteenth, seventeenth, and eighteenth centuries there are numerous accounts of these elections in manuscripts in the Correr and Marciana libraries in Venice. Most of these begin by naming the leading candidates and then list the men voted on in each ballot, with the number of votes each received.[52] From these accounts it is clear that the number of leading candidates declined in the period under study. In the sixteenth century there were always three or four men who were outstandingly *dogabile,* and behind them were perhaps another ten men who were worthy enough to be nominated and to receive ten or fifteen votes in the balloting. In the seventeenth century there were usually about two leading candidates. But in the eighteenth usually only one nobleman was outstanding by virtue of his experience, ability, eloquence, and wealth.

The way in which the nobility accepted new families in the seventeenth and eighteenth centuries is perhaps the clearest evidence of the growing seriousness of the problem under discussion. The speeches in the Great Council and the way the families were ennobled show that the lack of men had become far more worrisome at the end of that period than it had been at the beginning of it. The next chapter deals in detail with the creation of new noble families, but this much can be said here: When new families were ennobled during the seventeenth and early eighteenth century, the principal motive was to collect " entrance fees " from the new families and use the money for a war chest. The need to replace families which had died out and to have more men to hold expensive and important offices was considered a secondary motive, even though some nobles saw the need for new men clearly and seem to have been sincere in urging it as a reason for accepting new families. On the other hand, when in 1774 and 1775 a five-man commission urged the Great Council to offer the status of Venetian nobility to forty aristo-

[52] Correr, Cic. 2479, 2480, 3647; Marc., It. VII, 307 (8467), and some information from DaMosto, *I dogi* (pp. 288, 293-94, 298, 307, 311, 317-18) for some eighteenth-century elections. There are interesting accounts of the elections of 1501, 1521, and 1523 in Sanuto, *I diarii.*

Meeting of the Great Council of Venice

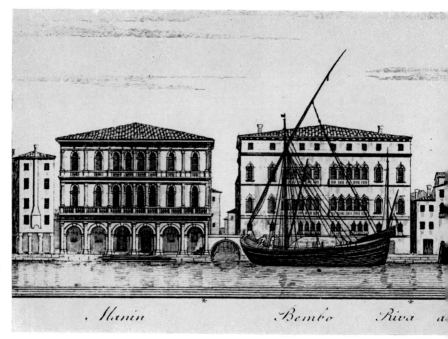

Manin and Bembo Palaces, near Rialto Bridge

Villa Grimani along the Brenta River on the mainland

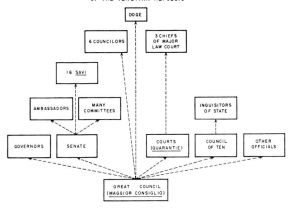

SIMPLIFIED DIAGRAM OF GOVERNMENT OFFICES
OF THE VENETIAN REPUBLIC

The doge, councilors, and three chiefs of the major law court made up the *Signoria*. The *Pien Collegio* consisted of the *Signoria* and the *savi*.

The arrows in the diagram indicate which government bodies were responsible for the election of others.

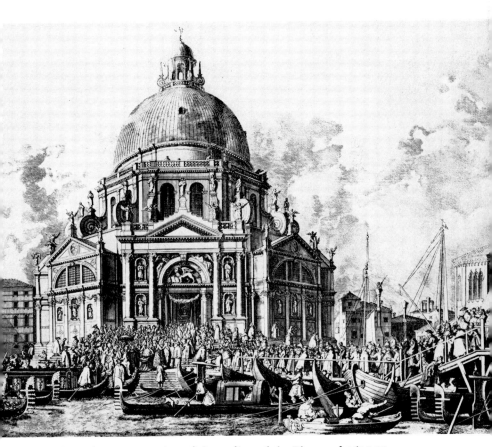

Annual commemoration of the ending of the Plague of 1630-31

303]   A MANPOWER SHORTAGE IN THE GOVERNMENT   97

cratic families from the mainland, there is no doubt that their only motive was to replace families that were dying out with families with enough wealth so that they could take a useful part in the government.

From the speeches of the five "correctors" it appears that the situation in 1775 was very serious. The lack of men was felt most acutely in the governorships and, it appears, in the embassies. There had been a "very serious deterioration" in the number of men who could afford these, and in 1774 there were "few— very few—families who could bear these burdens." For many of the other posts which required ability and willingness to work, but did not confer a great deal of honor, there were very few candidates. One of the correctors mentioned that twenty-five years earlier when his father had competed for a place in one or the other of the government commissions which supervised the Venetian grain supply and the execution of sentences by civil courts (*Biave* and *Atti*) there had been 125 or 130 other men who wanted posts on the committees. In the 1770's there were only thirty-four or thirty-five who wanted them. The decline in the number of competitors fed on itself; everyone tended to lose interest in competing for a position if there was little competition for it and, consequently, little honor in winning it. Furthermore, it was often necessary to elect the only man who offered himself as a candidate for an office. Significantly there were very few young men who now competed for the office of *savio ai ordeni*, which was a traditional first rung on the ladder for one bent on a political career. Frequently it was necessary to elect the same men over and over to the office. The correctors were circumspect in discussing the question of the most important offices of the government. They were themselves members of the *collegio* and could hardly be expected to declare outright that there were not enough able candidates for the posts they held. But Pietro Barbarigo did imply that while there was no lack of candidates for the most important offices, it would be a good thing if there were a wider selection of suitable men from whom to choose.[53]

In discussing the decline of the nobility, the corrector, Alvise

[53] Balbi, *Relazione delle cose,* pp. 171-99, 214-25, 271.

Zen, pointed out a danger which had perhaps never seemed so threatening before. If the nobility continued to decline as it was doing, he said, there was great danger that the government would become oligarchic. The Great Council included all the adult noblemen and was the sovereign authority in the Republic. It had continued through Venetian history to maintain the power balance between different organs of the government such as the Senate, Council of Ten, and the *Quarantie* because its meetings were attended not only by members of those bodies but also by a large number of " disinterested " nonoffice holders. When questions arose as to the constitutional powers of the different bodies, these disinterested persons could always be counted on to judge impartially and to give fair votes which kept any one body from exceeding its powers. Zen broke down the membership of the Great Council as follows: There were 280 senators, 17 members of the Council of Ten, and 120 in the *Quarantie*. This made a total of 420. In addition there was a considerable number in other offices in the city, and about 250 who were always absent from the Great Council because they were employed in governing cities and islands, commanding ships, and serving as ambassadors. Finally, there were the " disinterested " nobles who were not included in these groups. Zen pointed out how the Great Council had rapidly declined during the previous couple of centuries and said that in his own time there were usually only about 850 men at Great Council meetings. He implied that there was still a sufficiently large number of disinterested nobles to keep the balance between government bodies. But he predicted that in about twenty years there would be only about 350 present at meetings, in which case there would no longer be enough men to settle constitutional disputes. The result would be anarchy between the organs of government; and the Senate with its adherents would be large and powerful enough to control the Great Council. The Senate, he said, might rule well in these circumstances, but its authority would be illegitimate and, furthermore, a few men might then seize control. According to a note in the margin of the account of these speeches, Zen wept while he described the danger and urged the Great Council to avoid this awful fate.[54] It may be that Zen was correct in visualizing the danger of oligarchy as the most serious possible consequence of the diminishing of the Venetian nobility. Since the Republic fell only twenty-three years later, the question was never resolved.

At the beginning of the discussions of the proposals to ennoble new families, most of the Great Council was bitterly opposed to the plan. This opposition was based on snobbishness, traditionalism, and fear on the part of the poor nobles that they would face greater competition for the small but lucrative offices. (See Chapter V.) The fact that the Great Council finally agreed to accept the new families confirms that the nobility recognized that the reduction of its numbers and the lack of wealthy members had created a really serious situation.

The burden of this chapter is that the decline of the nobility in numbers and wealth—the loss many times multiplied of families like the Valiers and Basegios—caused a critical lack of nobles capable of filling important offices. To say this partly contradicts a charge of oligarchy which has frequently been levelled against the Venetian nobility. Perhaps the French historian Daru, who wrote a history of Venice which was intended to justify Napoleon's conquest of the Republic, was the most vocal of those who have claimed that toward the end of the Republic's life a small group of nobles monopolized the chief offices of the government and constituted a real oligarchy.[55] If this was indeed the case throughout the seventeenth and eighteenth centuries, then there is little sense in talking about a " manpower shortage " in the ruling class. A shortage can be said to have existed only if men were actually needed, and they were not needed if a small group of men sought to keep the offices for themselves. At least they were not needed from the point of view of the oligarchs.

My feeling is that the oligarchic nature of the nobility has been overstressed. As I will try to show, it is true there was a

[54] Balbi, *Relazione delle cose,* pp. 171-81. The preamble of the law which was passed (A.S.V., *Colombo,* fols. 250-52) says that the addition of new families will assure that the Great Council will continue to be the custodian of the constitution.

[55] Pierre Antoine N.B. Daru, *Histoire de la république de Venise* (8 vols., Paris: Didot, 1821), VI, Chap. 39.

tendency in the later eighteenth century on the part of some families to try to monopolize certain key government offices. But this was late in the period under study and limited in scope. In any case, concurrent with the supposed oligarchic tendency there was an increasing recognition in the ruling class of the seriousness of the problem caused by the lack of qualified officeholders. This has already been demonstrated.

There was plently of resentment against the *grandi*—the wealthy and powerful—before and during the eighteenth century, but generally the charges made against them were not that they tried to monopolize the principal offices. The stormy episode centering around Renier Zen in the early seventeenth century is interesting in this respect. Zen was an able nobleman of average means who had a record of useful service, including one embassy to Rome. His fight against the *grandi,* or at least some of them, began when he publicly denounced the way the sons of the wealthy doge, Giovanni Corner, accepted offices and church benefices from which Venetian laws barred them. Events reached a dramatic high point when the Council of Ten tried to imprison or banish the fiery Zen and when a son of the doge ambushed and nearly killed him. The episode had something of an anticlimax in an ineffective " reform " of the Council of Ten in 1628. Zen was backed by the poor nobles and, it appears from the number of votes in his favor on some occasions, a considerable number of other patricians. From accounts of this episode, it does not appear that he and his followers accused the wealthy *grandi* of keeping a tight monopoly over the most important offices. What they did object to was the way the *grandi* used the power they had—especially in the Council of Ten—to favor other wealthy nobles, and the *grandi's* unfairness in their treatment of the poorer men. It is true that the poor nobles wanted to see some of their number in the Ten, and for this purpose they tried unsuccessfully to have a law enacted making the three chiefs of the *Quarantia* automatically members of the Ten.[56]

---

[56] Cozzi, *Il doge Nicolò Contarini,* p. 261. Cozzi cites Correr, Cic. 3274, *Raccolta di memorie storiche ed anecdote per formar la storia dell'Eccelso Consiglio dei dieci,* MS, " Scrittura di Z. A. Venier relative alli motivi per li quali nacquero le cose antescritte." pp. 152 ff. For summaries of the Zen episode see Cozzi's work and Romanin, *Storia documentata,* VII, Chap. 5.

The purpose, however, was not to break the monopolistic hold of a small group over this office, but to insure equal justice. If their purpose had been to destroy the oligarchical position of a few families, they would probably have attacked the *savi grandi*, the ducal councilors, and other government officers as well.

Some other charges which were made—often irresponsibly—against the *grandi* in this century were that they monopolized the most *lucrative* offices, spent the least possible money when they represented the state on embassies and in governorships, and held down the pay of the modest offices which provided a livelihood for poorer nobles.[57] But it was rarely if ever claimed before the end of the eighteenth century that there was a small group of nobles who jealously held on to such leading positions as doge, *savio grande*, ducal councilor, and member of the Ten, and rigorously excluded others from them.

In a book written in 1792, a " new " Venetian nobleman named Leopoldo Curti made a more detailed attack on the wealthy and powerful nobles and put heavy stress, as no one before him seems to have done, on the way a small number of families kept the principal offices in their possession. He claims that in looking over the lists of *savi grandi* and *savi di terra ferma* he discovered that these posts were held by members of only one-tenth of all the noble families—less than that, if he ruled out a few exceptional cases. Curti suggests that a policy of a few families of consciously excluding from important offices able men who did not belong to their group began in the seventeenth century but was practiced most in his own lifetime.[58] He says that the old families exaggerated the expenses of political careers, dwelt on the incapacity of others (sometimes real, because of lack of means to pay for education), bribed capable men outside their group with the offer of lesser but well-paid offices and used other means, some parliamentary and others not, for the purpose of " concentrating in their hands the exercise of all power, and all authority." [59]

[57] See Cozzi, *Il doge*, p. 247; and *Relazione della Serenissima*. The latter is devoted principally to complaints about the *grandi*.

[58] Leopoldo Curti, *Memorie storiche e politiche sopra la Repubblica di Venezia scritte l'anno 1792 da Leopoldo Curti* (2 pts.; Venice: Parolaris, 1812), pt. II, pp. 1-14, 67n., 153. On Curti's life and book, see Critical Note 3.

[59] *Memorie storiche,* pt. II, p. 70.

Curti's contention is partly borne out by the statistics presented earlier in this chapter in Table 1. As this table shows, if one considers the number of men who held office four times or more, there was a decline until the beginning of the eighteenth century, followed by a slight rise. The figures are: 1560-69—*35;* 1635-44 —*24;* 1731-40—*17;* and 1780-89—*23.* Perhaps because the figures are small the slight rise at the end is statistically insignificant, but I believe it is not. If the decline in the numbers down through the 1730's indicates fewer members of the inner ruling group, the rise at the end of the eighteenth century should show that the ruling group was then increasing. But this is incomprehensible, since during this time the nobility continued to decrease and there were no new opportunities to make wealth, and no new developments which would have fostered more public spirit on the part of the nobles. How can one account for the rise between 1740 and 1780? It appears that Curti's contentions explain it neatly. According to Curti, the *grandi* were most anxious to keep in their power the offices of *savio grande* and the Council of Ten. (This is understandable. The *savi* had great power over all the activities of the *Collegio* and the Senate, while the Council of Ten still had authority and elected two of the three feared *inquisitori di stato.*) If one counts the men who served four or more times in a decade in these two offices only, he gets the figures *21, 19, 15, 18.* These results indicate that it was repeated service in these two offices that caused the rise between 1740 and 1780. (There is no important change in the number of men elected to the somewhat less important office of ducal councilor.) What Curti has to say about the oligarchical activities of the *grandi* during his time fits in quite well with the figures. It appears that in the latter eighteenth century there may indeed have been an effort by some families to hold on to two important offices.

What Curti has to say should nevertheless be taken with more than a grain of salt. In the first place, neither the figures of Table 1 nor testimony by commentators during the seventeenth and eighteenth centuries confirms that there was any real attempt by a group of families to keep a tight grip on offices *before* the lat-

ter eighteenth century.[60] Even in Curti's time, Pindemonte claimed
that in continually electing *savi* from certain families the Senate
was a sheep which always clung to "inveterate habit." He does
not speak of an oligarchic monopoly of power.[61] Curti himself
admits, moreover, that the wealth and superior education of the
grandi made it almost inevitable that they should hold power[62]
and he also admits that there was in his time a deficiency of
worthy candidates.[63] In any case, Curti's harsh statements about
the *grandi* are a bit suspect. As a new noble and one who had
fled from Venice when under investigation by the inquisitors of
state for "abuse of power," he may have nursed a resentment
against the ruling group. Furthermore, some contemporaries completely refute what Curti has to say. One impoverished nobleman is supposed to have written after the fall of the Republic:
"If I had had ability, force, and education I could have risen to
the highest offices of authority—but not of profit—such as Senator, *Avogadore,* and even the Council of Ten and Inquisitor of
State, as I have seen some of my unfortunate group gloriously
succeed in doing during my time."[64] This testimony may deserve
no more credit than Curti's, but it shows that witnesses can be
found on both sides.

A summary of the points made in this chapter may be useful.
My principal aim has been to show the effects of the changes in
the nobility which were described earlier. As the ruling class
became smaller and the number of wealthy men decreased, there
were ever fewer men qualified and willing to fill the numerous
expensive and responsible offices of the Venetian government.
Luxurious living standards and political apathy also played a
part. It appears that the problem first became serious during the
1630's and was an important reason, although not the principal
one, which impelled the aristocracy to ennoble new families dur-

[60] One exception is the attempt by the *case ducali* to monopolize the dogeship,
but this had ended long before and had different motivations.

[61] Pindemonte, *op. cit., loc. cit.*

[62] *Memorie storiche,* pt. II, pp. 1-2.

[63] *Ibid.,* p. 69.

[64] Quoted in Romanin, *Storia documentata,* IX, 7n. He says the sentence comes
from a letter written by a *barnabotto* (poor nobleman) to Leonardo Giustiniano
Lolin after the fall of the Republic and cites *Lettera apologetica sulla Repubblica
di Venezia.* I have not been able to find the *Lettera.*

ing the seventeenth and early eighteenth centuries. The lack of
men became obvious first and was always most acute in elections
to the expensive embassies and governorships. Because of the
" manpower shortage," difficulty arose also in finding men of
sufficient maturity for all of the responsible offices; as time
passed these had to be given only too often to very young men.
Most serious of all, the core of the ruling class, able and public-
spirited nobles who served year-in, year-out in the most important offices, decreased rapidly so that direction of government
affairs was no longer always in the hands of experienced and
respected statesmen. There is some evidence of an effort by a
few families to allow none but their own members to serve as
savi grandi or in the Council of Ten, but even if true, this applied
only to these two offices and only during the last decades of the
Republic's existence. The discussions in 1774 and 1775 of the
plan to accept new families into the nobility for the expressed
and sole purpose of having more men who could hold offices
and the adoption of this proposal by the Great Council shows
how serious a problem the diminishing of the ruling class had
become by the end of the eighteenth century.

Other eighteenth-century governments may also have been
struggling with the problem of having too few competent councilors and civil servants, though little is known about this. As a
tendency developed to close the various parlements and estates
to anyone not of noble birth, these bodies probably found themselves short of qualified men. The Parlement of Grenoble provides an interesting comparison with Venice. Because this parlement insisted on recruiting itself from its own sons (or from the
fourth generation of nobility), its standards declined. Noblemen
who had received the required law degrees for little or no work,
and men who had no interest in law or vocation for it, but simply lived idly on their country estates, became members of the
Parlement. Young men became councilors when they were under
the required age of twenty-five, and presiding judges when they
were under the required age of forty.[65] The case of Venice, true,
is somewhat different. The republic had for a long time restricted

[65] J. Egret, *Le Parlement de Dauphiné et les affaires publiques dans la deuxième
moitié du 18ᵉ siècle* (Grenoble and Paris, 1942), Vol. I, pp. 19-27, summarized in
Palmer, *Age of the Democratic Revolution*, pp. 76-77.

major offices to nobles and her problem arose only when the
nobility diminished. But if the upper classes in other parts of
Europe tended to decrease as they did in Venice (this is discussed in Chapter VI), then this, coupled with the tendency to
aristocratize the various parlements and estates, may have created
" manpower shortages " in many places. Did this happen? Were
these problems as serious and as obvious as they were in Venice?
If these shortages of men became acute did the kings or the
" constituted bodies " create new members as a remedy? These
questions have received little systematic study.

CHAPTER V

A REMEDY WHICH FAILS

If the Venetian nobility had been so constituted that it continually absorbed able and wealthy men, the serious lack of nobles
for government offices might never have developed. New families would have replaced the old ones which died out, and the
ruling class would have remained large and more effective. But
in Venice this process of change, normal to social classes in most
societies, had been artificaly prevented for 265 years. The aristocracy had become a closed body, admitting virtually no one.
During this time it developed carefully practiced methods of
safeguarding its purity, and it became convinced that only its
members had the right or capacity to rule. Not until 1646, and
then only with the greatest reluctance, did the nobility yield to
the necessity of ending its closed caste system.

    There was talk in Venice during the 1630's of granting Vene-
tian nobility to aristocratic families from the mainland in order
to replace Venetian families which had died out and, apparently, in order to have more men available to serve in important
offices.[1] As it happened, not these needs, but the urgent demand
for a war chest finally impelled the Republic to create new noble
families. When the War of Crete against the Turks broke out
in 1645, Venice found itself not only without allies, but also
without funds. Numerous means were used to raise money.
Priests were asked to assemble the men of their parishes and
urge them to make large contributions; minor lucrative offices
were sold; various forced loans, taxes, and duties were used. An
especially effective way to collect funds in the Baroque period
was to sell the honors and privileges which men prized so highly.
Thus young noblemen were permitted to enter the Great Council before reaching the required age in return for a fee, and
nobles were permitted to buy the once highly esteemed honor of

[1] See Chapter IV.

106

being procurator of St. Mark. Finally it was proposed to allow five subject families to purchase, at a cost of 60,000 ducats each, the privileges of nobility.[2]

Beyond a doubt this proposal was viewed chiefly as a step to raise funds for the war chest. The preamble of the bill [3] offered in the Great Council speaks specifically of the great threat posed by the Turkish aggression and the urgent need of funds to pay for defense costs. The speeches made for and against it gave primary stress to the need for war funds. Giacomo Marcello told the nobles, " He is mistaken who believes that with the usual means we can cope with the demands of a war . . . . a year of paying for the war has already depleted the money-boxes and proved a burden to the people. . . . We . . . must arrange matters so that payment for our soldiers shall not be lacking, nor food for our people; and also so that the State shall not be desolated, and our subjects oppressed." [4] Since the usual means would not suffice, it was necessary to resort to the desperate remedy of selling the rights and privileges of Venetian nobility.

But if the need for money was foremost and more convincing, some leading political figures saw that by accepting new families the Republic could also compensate for the loss of many families that had died out. The bill dealing with the proposed ennoblements mentions in addition to the war needs, the " present number of our nobility, continually diminishing " and the desirability of dealing with this problem in order to elect the best men to offices.[5] In his speech in favor of the bill, Marcello, as described in the preceding chapter, spoke fervently of the disappearance of patrician families and the danger that inferior men would have to be elected to principal offices. Even Angelo Michiel, who spoke against the bill, admitted the need of more men in the Great Council.

The speeches of Marcello and Michiel for and against ennobling new families throw light on the Venetian nobility's image of itself. Michiel's rambling discourse touched on all sorts of

---

[2] For means used to raise money for war costs, see *Bilanci generali*, Vol. I, sec. VIII.

[3] A.S.V., Great Council, March 4, 1646, *Marcus*, fols. 161v-162v.

[4] *Degl'istorici*, Nani, *Historia della repubblica Veneta*, p. 90.

[5] See Michiel's speech, below.

minor objections to accepting new families, but concentrated most heavily on the injury that ennoblements of new families would do to the character of the nobility. In the times of the barbarian invasions, he said, the men who settled in the Venetian islands (and later became nobles) were not the rich and powerful of north Italy but those who had in them the ancient Roman valor. They sought refuge not for themselves but for their religion and for liberty, and theirs was a nobility of valor which could not be bought for gold. It was still thus in the seventeenth century, Michiel said. "One can never be Noble by force of gold who was not born of good blood, and does not acquire it [nobility] with fine and brave deeds." It was valorous men that the Republic needed, not the rich low-born who could pay the required price. He warned the nobles that they did not weep over the loss of many former Venetian possessions in the Mediterranean the way their descendants would weep if "this unstained Virgin" were prostituted to the basest kind of people. He reminded the urban Venetian nobility (whose origins were in trade) of the exclusiveness of the nobles of the mainland (whose origins were feudal and seigneurial). Though now reduced to governing their cities under the supervision of Venice, the mainland aristocrats were proud of their titles, some of which dated from times when Venice consisted only of sand bars; they would never accept new men in their city councils for all the money in the world. Michiel admitted the need of new families to replace those that had died out, but he opposed accepting them for money payments under the stress of war. He preferred to see nobility granted as it had been long ago in the War of Chioggia—as a reward for valor and self-sacrifice.[6]

Marcello's rebuttal suggests that he had a much less exalted idea of the nature of Venetian nobility. The prime need was for a war chest, he said, and it would be foolish to have it written on their tombs that they had lost the Venetian empire merely

[6] There is more than one manuscript copy of the Michiel speech in the libraries of Venice. I have used that in Correr, PD 96. Naturally, there is no way to be sure that this is the speech exactly as Michiel delivered it. He had other more minor objections to the proposals, but with the exception of his fear that there might be an embarrassing dearth of candidates for nobility (see below), I have not enumerated them.

because they did not want to admit into the nobility men " whom the fortune of birth has not made equal to us." His willingness to increase the number of nobles in the interest of having more men to fill offices derived from a practical point of view. Essentially he viewed the nobility as a class of rulers. If their number declined, more nobles should be created because " so many Patricians are so many Priests of liberty. . . ."

How did the rest of the nobility react to the proposal? While one might expect the strongest opposition to come from the oldest and richest families, the bill was sponsored in the Senate and Great Council by nearly[7] the whole of the *Collegio*. This body included men from some of the most influential families: a Mocenigo, a Gradenigo, and a Corner. It may be that these men supported the measure only because the financial situation was desperate. The Senate first passed the bill, then voted to " suspend " it, and then voted to have the bill recorded as passed. Michiel later implied in his speech to the Great Council that the senators had more or less held their noses as they gave the third vote, approving the bill only so that the Great Council might have a chance to vote on such an important matter. The Great Council reacted more emphatically than the Senate. After hearing the arguments of Michiel and Marcello, 366 voted favorably, 140 indicated that they were not sure about the bill or wanted it revised, and 528 rejected it.[8] It may be, as a contemporary suggests, that the majority voted against the proposal because they had been convinced by an argument of Michiel that there might be an embarrassing lack of candidates who would pay the required 60,000 ducats.[9]

In any case, the rejection of the bill by the Great Council was far from being the end of the matter. The ironic outcome was that after rejecting a proposal to accept a mere five families, the Great Council over the next seven decades accepted a total of 127 families.[10] No general bill was ever passed authorizing con-

---

[7] The ducal councilor Paolo Caotorta spoke against the bill in the Senate.

[8] All of this information follows the official record in A.S.V., Great Council, March 4, 1646, *Marcus*, fols. 161v-162v.

[9] *Distinzioni segrete*, pp. 30-31.

[10] A.S.V., Misc. cod., 866, describes 127 families. Occasionally I have discovered references to a slightly higher or lower number, the result of including or not including certain families which combined to raise the 100,000 ducats.

cessions of nobility; instead, each family was admitted under a special bill, with final approval in the hands of the Great Council. How the admissions of all these families started is not clear; it may be that the first of the new families made a request for nobility at the invitation of members of the *Collegio,* and that others simply followed their example. All of the new families payed 100,000 ducats, not the originally proposed 60,000, and this may have moved the more hostile noblemen to accept the necessity of enlarging the nobility. One hundred thousand ducats was somewhat more than the annual income of the richest merchants among the new nobles, and it was more than twice the annual incomes of the richest of the old noble families. Obviously the fees could help greatly with the costs of war.

Nearly 80 families were ennobled before the admissions were halted in 1669 when the War of Crete ended. Half this number were later accepted between 1684 and 1704 because of the expenses of the War of Morea against the Turks. A few other families entered the nobility in 1717 and 1718.[11]

If many patricians found the idea of accepting new families distasteful, they also objected to the manner in which the new families were accepted. In the Chioggian war three centuries earlier, the basis for acceptance of a family was its contribution not only of money but also of personal service in the fighting, and only half of the applicants were accepted. But in the seventeenth and eighteenth centuries the only important requirement was money, and no one who could pay was rejected. A contemporary parodied the whole procedure: " There are two kinds of citizens here, the noble and the ignoble. The former and the latter are branches of the same tree; but the former have their names written in a golden book, and the latter have overlooked this. So the whole difference is in the book. There are some who, to correct this mistake of memory, decide to have their names inscribed, but then it is necessary to pay a considerable sum to the editor, and thus the golden book has become a silver book . ." [12]

[11] For the debates in 1684, see *Degl'istorici,* Foscarini, *Historia,* pp. 159-162; and *Degl'istorici,* Garzoni, *Istoria,* I, pp. 92-95.

[12] Molmenti (*Storia di Venezia,* III, 25 n.) cites as his source for this passage Angelo Gouday (with the collaboration of Giacomo Casanova), *L'espion Chinois,*

According to a contemporary, when the head of one of the new families went to Doge Molin's room to kiss the doge's vestments and present his request for nobility, he lost his courage; he was suddenly overwhelmed by his lack of merit for such an honor. "Do you have the 100,000 ducats?" Molin asked him. The man replied that he had. "That is all you need," Molin said.[13]

Of the families who entered the nobility in the seventeenth and early eighteenth centuries,[14] roughly three-fifths were merchants, one-fifth lawyers and chancery officials of the class of *cittadini originali*, and one-fifth nobles from the Venetian mainland.[15] If the merchants were the most numerous, they were also the least respected. Anonymous commentators remarked that the ennoblement of these families reminded them of Venice's enemies, the Turks, who made *visirs* of cooks and *pashas* of merchants. The families connected in one way or another with trade included bankers; wholesale merchants who dealt in cloth, wax, iron, meat, and military clothing; druggists; butchers; jewelers; a shovel manufacturer; a glass manufacturer; and a book publisher. About twenty dealt in silk and wool, a testimony to the prosperity of those industries: and a large number came from the thriving Venetian city of Bergamo. The merchants included a few very wealthy and respected families such as the Rezzonicos. This family had originally come to Venice from Como as agents of another merchant family, but soon surpassed their employers in wealth and were among the principal merchants of Italy. Descriptions of them state that they had always "lived nobly," were extremely wealthy, decorous, courteous, and respected. They were

---

ou l'envoyé secret de la Cour de Pekin, pour examiner l'état présent de l'Europe (Cologne, 1764).

[13] *Distinzioni segrete*, p. 27.

[14] Most of the information regarding the new families on this and the following pages comes from A.S.V., Misc. cod. 740 and 866; and Correr, Grad. 32. (See Critical Note 1.) For a collection of the families' requests for nobility, statements from the Venetian mint regarding the payment of the 100,000 ducats, decrees granting nobility, and a record of the voting on each family, see A.S.V., Avogaria del comun, b. 181/1 and 182/2.

[15] The statement that three-fifths of the new families were merchants is only an approximation. *Cittadini originali* had the right to trade in the same way the nobles did. It may be that some of those listed in the books of descriptions of families as *cittadini* were actually merchants rather than minor officials and it may be that some of those described as merchants also belonged to this class.

distant cousins of Pope Innocent XI. During the eighteenth cen-
tury a Rezzonico became a cardinal and finally Pope (Clement
XIII). The magnificent palace on the Grand Canal in which the
Rezzonicos lived is now a museum.

The majority of the merchants had humbler origins. Giulio
Veronese came from Verona and first lived by transporting goods
in his boat. He bought a fruit shop and at the same time began
to prosper in the business of carrying oil from ships to warehouses. Then he entered a partnership with other merchants and
went to Puglia, where he became an important merchant who
sent goods as far as Marseilles. In 1700, with his considerable
wealth, he was able to become a noble. Typical of the merchant
families who most scandalized the Venetian aristocracy when
they were ennobled were the Zolios, who had been pork butchers
in Verona. After coming to Venice and before becoming nobles,
they dealt in oil and soap and, according to contemporaries, they
could always be seen in their store wearing aprons. They were
ennobled in 1656. Like many other families, they seem to have
been much poorer as nobles than they had been as merchants—
the result of paying the stiff "entrance fee." According to one
writer, after they became nobles, the Zolios lived by holding
minor offices.

The *cittadini originali*—mostly government secretaries and lawyers—who joined the nobility were usually respected, able men,
often devoted to the government, and in some cases from ancient
Venetian families. The Franceschi, for example, had failed by
one vote to win nobility for their services in the War of Chioggia. The Ottobons could boast of an ancestor who had been in
command of a ship that had run a siege of Venetian forces by
the Turks in 1470, and three members of the family had been
elected to the highest office open to *cittadini,* that of grand chancellor. Marco Ottobon claimed in his request for nobility to have
made twenty-six trips or voyages in the service of the Republic,
in the years before he was elected grand chancellor. After Marco
became a noble, his son Peter became cardinal and later was
elected Pope, taking the name of Alexander VIII—impressive
evidence of the stature of this *cittadino* family. Giovanni Francesco Verdizzotti came from a much less distinguished family.

His father was a tailor and, as a boy, Giovanni earned money for his family by leading a blind man. Later he served as a *bravo,* or a kind of bodyguard, for quarrelsome noble families. His spirit impressed a member of the wealthy Pisani family who backed him when he entered the chancellory and he became *segretario alle voci.* He was as skilled at intrigue as he was at clerical work and this post, which dealt with elections to offices, seems to have provided a useful means for gaining noble adherents. To the surprise of many, he was next elected secretary of the Senate, defeating a more experienced and very respected man who had served as secretary of the Council of Ten. His failure, however, subsequently to be elected grand chancellor was a blow to his great ego, and he could only compensate for it, as he did, by raising the necessary money and becoming a nobleman. In contrast to the merchants, the *cittadini* who became nobles had been, in the words of a contemporary, " esteemed and powerful "; but as nobles, he said, they were less respected and the payments of 100,000 ducats had cost them much of their wealth.[16]

The nobles from the Venetian mainland were probably the group most welcome to the Venetian aristocracy. Perhaps a half-dozen of them came from families older than any in the Venetian patriciate.[17] The Gambaras and Brandolins could be traced back at least to the sixth and seventh centuries. The Valmaranas claimed descent from a Roman consul and had been made counts of Valmarana by the emperor Conrad II in 1031. Frequently these families could claim, in their requests for nobility, to have fought for the Republic in various wars against the Turks and against Austria. Cardinal Giovanni Francesco Gambara had backed the Republic rather than the Pope when Venice was put under an interdict at the beginning of the seventeenth century; this was a point in their favor forty years later when the Gambara brothers were ennobled.

If many of the new families lacked aristocratic graces and useful governmental experience, some of them at least were very wealthy. One anonymous writer claims that though a certain number had nearly impoverished themselves by paying the 100,-

[16] *Distinzioni segrete,* p. 30.
[17] *Ibid.,* p. 26.

000 ducats fee,[18] three of the new families had annual incomes
of 80,000 ducats, and three others were only slightly less wealthy;
in contrast, the three richest old families had incomes of 40,000
ducats.[19] There is no doubt that the ennoblements provided the
Republic with a considerable number of men who could afford
to fill expensive offices.

The new men seem to have been only moderately successful
in filling the gaps in the ruling class caused by the disappearance
of old families. One of the books of descriptions of the new
families mentions numerous men who served frequently and
willingly in expensive and undesired posts but never held the
positions of greatest responsibility and highest honor.[20] Government records show that new men were put on ordinary government committees and occasionally arrived in the Senate, became
captains of naval ships, and served in the governorships; but
until the last decades of the Republic they never served as *savi
grandi* or in the Council of Ten. No member of a new family
was ever elected ambassador to one of the five major courts—
Vienna, Rome, Paris, Madrid, and Constantinople.[21]

That the new families would not be used might have been
predicted. Part of the blame lay with the nobles of the old families, who deliberately excluded their new colleagues from the
most important offices. Antonio Ottobon told his son that " The
mere fact of being a new man will exclude you from the highest
offices of the government." [22] The old families were no doubt
partly justified if they wanted to keep the new men out of posts
for which they were not fitted. The author of a little seventeenth
century essay on the nobility explains that new men were kept
out of the key offices for reasons of " public decorum." [23] Many

[18] A.S.V., Misc. cod., 866 (one of the anonymous books of descriptions of the
new families) says of the Rizzi that they spent all they had to become nobles and
from being rich silversmiths became poor noblemen. The same kind of remark is
made in this source about a number of other families.

[19] *Relazione del anonimo* (in Molmenti, *Curiosità*), pp. 417-18.

[20] Correr, Grad. 32.

[21] For the names of men who served in almost all posts, see A.S.V., Segretario
alle voci, elections of Great Council and Senate. I checked the Senate elections,
regs. 16-26, for the names of ambassadors.

[22] Marc., It. VII, 2020 (9148), no pagination. This is a long, Polonius-like letter
of advice to the son.

[23] *Della nobilità veneta*, fol. 805v.

of the new nobles lacked the experience, polish, and prestige necessary for these posts. The Maffettis, a merchant family, illustrate this problem. Two brothers were described by a contemporary as having been " civilized " by living in Venice, while the others who had remained in the *rustichezza* of Bergamo were unpolished and hence the " plaything " of the political machinations of others. Naturally such men could not be useful public servants and the old-family nobles could be expected to see that they had no opportunity to bring discredit on the government. In many cases the old-family nobles may have wished to preserve the honorable and important offices for themselves simply because they enjoyed the possession of power. Leopoldo Curti maintained in 1792 that it had been justifiable for the old families to exclude the new ones from offices at first when the new men lacked experience, but it was because of simple greed for power that they continued this policy during subsequent generations. There were new men who had the necessary ability, prestige, and wealth, according to Curti; and in view of the " deficiency of worthy subjects," he considered their exclusion harmful to the Republic.[24]

The new families themselves were partly to blame if they did not immediately take up their share of important offices. The bulk of them were merchant families with no traditions of government service. Hence they lacked not only prestige and experience but also interest in taking part in government. They probably suffered also from feelings of inferiority. Others could not afford government service because, like the Zolio family, they had spent all they had in buying their new status and they now looked on trade as demeaning.[25] The descriptions of the new men suggest how their interests and habits prevented many of them from taking up their responsibilities. Some remained busy at trade in Venice or the provincial cities; others retired to their country villas and never appeared in Venice; some gambled

[24] Curti, *Memorie istoriche*, pt. II, pp. 69, 237-38.
[25] An unfortunate side effect of the ennoblements was that many important merchants deserted trade when they became nobles. Venetian economic life suffered as a result. See *Degl'istorici*, Garzoni, *Istoria della Repubblica*, I. p. 93, and the report of the papal nuncio Francesco Pannocchieschi published in Molmenti, *Curiosità*, pp. 313-14.

away their money, and one died in the bed of a prostitute. The new men tended to imitate the worst qualities of the old families.

There is some evidence that the new men were more inclined than the old-family nobles were to shirk their duty of service in the expensive governorships. Between 1738 and 1773, nobles from new families were elected about 25 percent of the time to governorships which carried a penalty for refusal,[26] but they made just under 33 percent of the requests for dispensations from these offices and they received *more* than a third of the sentences of banishment for outright refusal to serve in them.[27] There is more evidence leading to the same conclusion in a list of "Noblemen, who do not desire offices," conserved in the Correr library.[28] Apparently the list was drawn up in 1753 by a nobleman who was in some way responsible for, or interested in, the election of men to offices. The document makes it clear that the new families were apathetic about taking part in the government. Of 255 men who did not want offices, 122 belonged to new families. Thus, over half of the total number of new men did not want offices; in contrast, only 10 percent of the old nobility were not interested in government service.

Yet despite some lack of interest and experience and despite the opposition of the old families, the new nobles did eventually help in filling both the undesired and expensive offices and some of the most responsible and honorable ones. While they may have tried to avoid the offices such as governorships which carried a penalty for refusal, by 1775 they had served in 312 of these positions.[29] Lodovico Flangini was admiral of a Venetian fleet which fought the Turks in 1717; wounded by an arrow, Flangini had his sailors carry him to the bridge where he witnessed the end of the battle and the flight of the Turks, and

[26] I counted the new nobles who served in a sampling of these offices between 1738 and 1773. It may appear to be an injustice that they were elected to the unpopular governorships 25 percent of the time, when they only made up about 17 percent of the nobility; but wealthier men were customarily elected to these posts, and the new men were a little wealthier than the old family nobles.

[27] For the dispensations and banishments, see A.S.V., Avogaria del comun, reg. 616/1 and b. 3580. The family most often punished by banishments for refusals of offices was the Widman family, one of the three mentioned earlier that had incomes of 80,000 ducats at one point in the seventeenth century.

[28] Correr, Donà, 445.

[29] Balbi, *Relazione delle cose*, p. 279.

then died a hero's death. The first new-family noble to serve as a Venetian general received that post in the final years of the eighteenth century.[30] Even the central offices of ducal councilor, *savio grande,* and the Council of Ten finally opened to the new men. Only two of their group served in these positions in the decade from 1731 to 1740. But between 1780 and 1789, twenty-five new-family nobles served in these offices.[31] (Many of these, however, were ducal councilors, who had less authority than the *savi grandi* and members of the Ten.) The most impressive demonstration of this assimilation of the new men into the important posts is provided by Lodovico Manin. His ancestors had been counts in Friuli before they were ennobled in 1651. According to one source, after they joined the Venetian nobility they spent enormous sums building magnificent churches and palaces in Venice and on the mainland, and they spent heavily in offices to which they were elected. Like so many others, they were not soon given any honorable posts of great responsibility, yet with time they solidified their position in the nobility. Born in 1725, Lodovico Manin married well, held important governorships and financial positions, and received the honor of election as procurator of St. Mark. His great wealth must have helped him as he progressed through these offices. In 1789 he became the first (and, of course, the last) member of a new family to become a doge.[32] That there was still prejudice against the new families is evident in a well-known remark attributed to one of Manin's competitors: "They have made a Friulian doge; the Republic is dead." As events turned out, he was right.

Although the new nobles did take up some of the burden of expensive and even of responsible offices, their acceptance could only arrest, not halt, the decline in the number of Venetian patri-

[30] Pindemonte, untitled essay on the decadence of the Venetian government, p. 350. The noble was Carlo Widman.

[31] Curti (*Memorie istoriche,* II, 237-38) claims that the new families entered the *Collegio* despite opposition from the old families, because the difference in number between the two groups diminished and the new nobles gained enough voting power to put themselves in office. But actually the percentage of new nobles remained fairly stable—about 17 percent—throughout the eighteenth century. It seems more likely either that they were accepted by the old families, or formed an alliance with the poorer families of that group.

[32] Da Mosto, *I dogi,* pp. 316-21.

cians. Chapter III described how the nobility declined in size from 2,500 or 2,600 nobles in the mid-sixteenth century to 1,600 a hundred years later when the ennobling of new families started. Even after the seemingly prodigal conferment of nobility on 127 families, the patriciate was larger by only 100 men seventy years later when the ennoblements ceased.[33] Why had there been such a paltry gain? For one reason, the old nobility was moving fast on its suicidal course; avoidance of marriage was accounting for the disappearance of many families. Then too, the new families were not great " clans " as the Corners and Contarini had been. A number consisted of elderly men—brothers—only one of whom was married. Furthermore, the new families seem to have died out as fast as the old.[34] In 1684, only fifteen years after the end of the first wave of acceptance of new families, Foscarini observed that many of them had already disappeared;[35] of the total of 127 families, thirty-seven had disappeared by 1775. To compensate for the decline of the nobility, it would have been necessary continually to add large numbers of newcomers. But the ennoblements were suspended in 1718, and (as was shown in Chapter III) the size of the nobility plunged from about 1,700 in that year to 1,300 in 1775, to 1,100 at the fall of the Republic in 1797.

Only in 1775, two decades before the fall of the Republic, did the nobility really confront the problem caused by its decrease and agree to accept new families for the sole purpose of making itself more effective as a ruling class. In the previous year the Great Council had elected a commission of five " correctors " to propose laws dealing with a number of abuses.[36] With eight months at their disposal, the correctors had begun by successfully recommending the closing of the Ridotto, or casino, where

[33] There were 1,710 nobles (aged 25 or over) in 1719. (Correr P.D. 5b.)

[34] Beltrami (*Storia della popolazione,* p. 78) shows that the number of *cittadini originali,* like that of the nobles, declined during the last centuries of the Republic; similarly (p. 77) the nobles of the mainland declined at least during the last half of the eighteenth century. If this decline took place among Venetian and mainland nobility and *cittadini originali,* it is not surprising if it also happened with the new nobles.

[35] See his speech, cited in Chapter III, fn. 44.

[36] On the correctors and their work in general, see Romanin, *Storia documentata,* VIII, pp. 200-11.

many men had gambled away their wealth. They had then written a decree raising salaries paid in a number of government
offices and composed legislation designed to restrain the power
of the *savi grandi* and make the *Collegio* and Senate work harder.
Then, to the surprise and dismay of most of the nobility, they
recommended a decree offering nobility to forty new families.[37]

This time the requirements which it was proposed should be
enforced in accepting new families were carefully adjusted to
the prejudices of the nobility and to the needs which the new
families had to fill. Most important, the new families had to
show that they had possessed some title of nobility over four
generations. (Presumably they would be old aristocratic families
from the Venetian mainland.) At intervals between 1646 and
1718 the Venetian nobility had accepted despised merchant families and *cittadini originali,* but then there had been a pistol at
their heads; the needs of war had made the 100,000-ducat fees
indispensable. Before the War of Crete in the 1630's, the Venetians had talked of accepting aristocratic families from the mainland, and even during the war when Venice was accepting any
family able to pay the fee, one nobleman urged several times that
the Republic should only admit aristocratic families.[38] The books
of descriptions of the new families indicate that the writers preferred those new families that were of aristocratic origin. In the
1740's a committee responsible for government revenues reported
that it hoped there might be some noble families in the subject
cities who could help to balance the budget by paying the customary 100,000 ducats; the committee made no mention of accepting merchant families or even *cittadini originali.*[39] Thus when
the correctors wrote their proposed decree in 1774, there was a
climate of opinion like that in an exclusive club which has had
to admit newly-rich members for the sake of their entrance fees.
Without the pressure of a financial emergency, the inclination
was toward stricter entrance requirements. When the correctors
spoke in favor of the bill in front of the Great Council,[40] they

[37] Feb. 12, 1774, A.S.V., Great Council, *Colombo,* fols. 245v-248v.
[38] *Relazione della Serenissima,* p. 25.
[39] Report of deputati ed agg. alla prov. del danaro pub., Oct. 1, 1745, *Bilanci generali,* II, p. 435.
[40] Most of my information on the arguments for and against the bill comes from Nicolò Balbi, *Relazione delle cose.*

left this prejudice in favor of the noble families unexpressed—
and wisely so, in view of the fact that the Council included men
descended from ennobled merchant families—but explained that
it was considered wiser not to accept merchants this time lest
they damage the economy by giving up trade and discourage the
desired aristocratic families from applying for membership in the
Venetian nobility.

Another requirement which was designed to insure that the
new families should really become useful to the government was
that they have incomes of 10,000 ducats a year. The correctors
felt that this income would be enough to enable a family to
accept and do justice to the more expensive offices. The new
families were not required to pay the 100,000 ducats previously
requested. It is true that this time there was no urgent need for
funds, but the abandonment of this condition for membership
does show how serious the patriciate considered the need for new,
aristocratic, and reasonably wealthy men. Probably only rich merchants, now considered unsuitable, could have payed large sums
to enter the nobility. Experience, furthermore, had shown the
harm of bleeding families of all their wealth while granting them
membership in the nobility.

The most interesting aspect of the proposal is that it was intended to deal more or less permanently with the shrinking process by systematically compensating for the annual decrease in
the number of nobles. As the correctors explained it, they had
calculated that the Great Council was decreasing at a rate of
ten men a year. If forty families were ennobled over twenty
years, as the proposed decree stipulated, and if they averaged five
men apiece, this would just compensate for the annual decrease.
The bill seems to have been intended as a permanent solution to
the problem of a decreasing nobility. If accepted and effective, it
would amount to changing the Venetian nobility from a caste
which only occasionally accepted new members under pressure to
a "flexible" aristocracy with a built-in system of replenishment.
The bill as originally proposed at the end of 1774 contained
a recommendation at the end that it be renewed at the end of
twenty years. Probably in deference to the conservatism of some

of the opponents, this passage was stricken from the bill when it was reintroduced in the Great Council a few weeks later.[41]

Such a radical plan was bound to create lively dissension. According to one noble who wrote an account of these events, he had never heard such widespread disapproval of proposed legislation as was expressed after the first reading of the bill. There was vehement discussion of the proposal during the following week, and at the next meeting of the Great Council almost seven hours of speech-making preceded the voting on the plan. The correctors doggedly explained the reasoning behind the decree and tried to persuade the nobility to vote for it. Their principal argument centered on the lack of men for offices. This is a matter already discussed at length in Chapter IV; suffice it to say they pointed out that the new nobles would have incomes which would permit them to bear some of the burden of the expensive and undesired governorships and that they would provide a larger field of choice in elections to the most important offices. This argument probably had the largest appeal to nobles with average wealth. As was mentioned in the previous chapter, the correctors also claimed that if the Great Council continued to diminish in size, there was a serious danger that it would no longer have enough non-office-holding members who could disinterestedly arbitrate between other bodies such as the Senate and the *Quarantie*. In a very small Great Council, members of the Senate and their adherents might dominate proceedings and turn the Republic into a virtual oligarchy.[42]

The arguments of the opponents of the bill were on the whole petty and easily refuted. They were based mainly on the fear (of poorer nobles) that some of the new men might compete with them for the minor lucrative offices, and on a widespread dislike of admitting new men into the ranks. One adversary pointed out that if the nobility was shrinking in numbers this process could be arrested if the nobility would not put a selfish desire to

---

[41] Mar. 19, 1775, Great Council, A.S.V., *Colombo*, fols. 250-52.

[42] Balbi, *Relazione delle cose*, pp. 158-60, 171-99, 214-30, 261-82. The second bill (Mar. 19, 1775) hints in its preamble at the oligarchical danger, but omits mention of the difficulty of finding candidates for offices. The discussions make it clear, however, that this was the more important motivation for the proposal.

live well before their duty to marry and have children, and he insolently pointed out that the five correctors were themselves guilty of " letting their conspicuous Families miserably perish." [43] But the adversaries of the bill deserved a better hearing than they received when they warned that there might not be forty families on the mainland who were interested in becoming Venetian nobles. Alvise Zen answered that if in the past men had willingly paid 100,000 ducats to become Venetian nobles, they would be all the more anxious to do so when they were required to pay nothing at all. He told his opponents that theirs was a " petty and miserable " argument. [44]

The general hostility to the plan was slow to dissolve. Opposition speakers were warmly applauded while the excellent speech of Zen in support of the bill was twice interrupted by " murmuring." At the end of nearly seven hours of discussion at the first meeting, the voting was held amid tumultuous clapping and banging. On two ballots the required number of votes was not cast, so the decree was tabled for five weeks until the correctors made revisions in it. Most of the same arguments were used again in speeches at the next meeting when the bill was reconsidered. The final speech was made by the corrector Lodovico Flangini, himself a member of a " new " family ennobled in 1664. After carefully reviewing the arguments in favor of the plan, Flangini asked his listeners to imagine that they were the defenders of a besieged city. If friends came to help them at the very moment the enemy was breaking down the gates, no one would cry, " No, No. We don't want them here. We would have to pay them. The fewer there are of us the better." In the same way, he said the nobility would be reckless if they turned down this opportunity to add to their number before it was too late. Flangini's speech made a strong impression; the Great Council was finally and reluctantly persuaded by the truth of the correctors' arguments, [45] and the proposal to ennoble forty families was approved.

[43] Balbi, *Relazione delle cose*, p. 248. It appears from the *Libri d'Oro* that, as was implied, not one of the five correctors was married. The corrector who spoke next called the adversary's point " a base device to curry favor for his own opinion."

[44] Balbi, *Relazione delle cose*, pp. 158-214.

[45] Balbi, *Relazione delle cose*, pp. 261-87.

The sequel was an anticlimax. As predicted by opponents of the bill, there were not forty noble families of the mainland who wished to become Venetian nobles. Only ten families applied and met the requirements to enter the nobility.[46] As required by the law, they were families which could produce documentary evidence of noble status. It goes without saying that in the two decades of life remaining to the Republic, they had no opportunity to reach any positions of distinction there.

One of the more interesting of this group was the Pindemonte family which claimed to have been driven out of Pistoia centuries before in some civic upheaval and to have scattered, some to the States of the Church, some to the Kingdom of Naples, and some to the Veneto. Giovanni Pindemonte was a colorful figure, a poet with democratic ideas, who came to Venice after the family had been ennobled, was elected to the Senate, and served honorably as *podestà* in Vicenza. Later he was jailed for eight months after he struck the angry husband of a *borghesa* he had trifled with; bitterness over this imprisonment seems to have reinforced his democratic ideas and he began to speak out against the aristocratic government which he had willingly joined. He fled to France, then returned and in 1796 wrote a witty essay on the decadence of the Venetian government. Later he took part in the government of Italy under Napoleon.[47]

Why did more aristocrats of the mainland not take advantage of the apparently generous offer to become part of the Venetian nobility? A French ambassador reported that the old aristocratic families of the mainland despised the families who had been ennobled by Venice after 1646, since these were of low birth and had simply bought nobility with cash: the mainland families had no desire to mix with such people. Furthermore, they preferred to remain fairly inactive in their own cities instead of going to Venice and having to serve in offices of only moderate

[46] They were Borini, Buzzacarini, Caiselli, Martinengo, Musatti, Ottolin, Pindemonte, Spineda, Trento, and Zoppola. For most of the relevant documents or copies thereof, see A.S.V., Dep. ed agg. alla prov. del danaro pub., b. 560-74.

[47] See Biadego's account of Pindemonte's life in the preface to *Poesie e lettere* and the *supplica* of the Pindemontes in Correr, Lazzari, 73.

importance.[48] Whatever their reasons, their apathy toward the offer must have been a terrible blow to Venetian pride.[49]

While the decision in 1775 to accept new families seemed at first to imply a great change in the aristocratic system, and to offer a solution to the problem of finding enough suitable noblemen for offices, it changed nothing and solved nothing. The system and the problem had their roots too deep in the past. The nobility had been a closed body since the fourteenth century, and it had developed its form and mentality at a time when it did not need new men. Even when the nobility accepted a fairly large number of new families in the decades after 1646, it did not agree to the principle of systematically replenishing its numbers. Involved in costly wars with the Turks, it accepted the new families only because of the fees they paid. The nobility did not then work out a system, any more than it had in previous centuries, of gradually accepting suitable new men as they were needed to replace families that were impoverished or had died out.

The damage had been done by 1775. True, the nobility then was finally convinced of the desirability of at least compensating for any future decline in its size. But the reckless and almost cynical custom practiced earlier of accepting any family that could pay 100,000 ducats had resulted in an influx of families of all kinds of backgrounds. Many of these were considered a discredit to the noble class, and it was apparently mainly for this reason that the aristocratic families on the Venetian mainland turned down the invitation to join the nobility when it was extended in 1775. Even if the desired mainland families had been attracted by the offer, they could hardly have compensated for

[48] Berengo (*Società veneta*, pp. 14-15n.) cites as the source of these remarks, Archives des affaires étrangères, Paris, Correspondence politique, Venise, Vol. 247, fols. 94v-95r (dispatch of 23 Jan. 1790); and Vol. 250, fols. 368v-369r (*Notice sur l'état de Venise*, 1793).

[49] In 1797, when the advancing French were already in the Veneto, Daniele Dolfin urged the Senate to permit the subject cities to elect about twenty citizens to represent them at Venice and become life-time members of the Venetian aristocracy. He said that this would gain the love and support of the mainland subjects. The *savi grandi* later reported to the Senate that the proposal was inopportune and might cause harmful and tempestuous discussions in the Great Council. (A.S.V., Senato terra ferma militare, p. 43; and anonymous, *Memoria che può servire alla storia degli ultimi otto anni della Repubblica di Venezia* [London: Elvington, 1798], pp. 217-18.)

the past depletion of the nobility and restored this body to the point where it could fill the principal offices with good administrators. The number needed was too great. At best they could have prevented a future decline. As it was, their refusal meant that the shrinking process was to continue. Between 1775 and 1797 the nobility diminished by about 200 men.

If Venice had been left undisturbed, this decline would soon have led to a mortal paralysis of the government. Before that could happen, however, there came the whirlwind of the French Revolution. Obeying the command of Napoleon, the nobles of Venice dissolved their Republic.

CHAPTER VI

SOME IMPLICATIONS OF THIS STUDY

It seems certain that the Republic of Venice would have expired in 1797 even if her nobility had not become unequal to the tasks of government. Even if there had been, as there were 300 years earlier, 2,500 noblemen instead of 1,200, and if all of these had been rich, able, and as determined as the greatest Venetian heroes—Carlo Zeno, Andrea Gritti, Francesco Morosini —Napoleon would still have conquered the anachronistic city state. Centuries before Napoleon's time, powerful territorial states had overtaken and surpassed Venice in almost every field of competition. It would not be true to say, then, that Venice finally collapsed because of the demographic and economic decline of her nobility. Rather, the growing incapacity of the nobility for its governing task is a part of a general decline of Venice— one which involved not only local government and the Republic's place in the political sun of Europe, but also her empire, her economy, her artistic production, the stature of her university, and even the fervency of her religious spirit. What had earlier given the Republic vitality, coherence, and a sense of mission slowly waned during her last centuries.

Some of the social changes which took place in Venice form part of a pattern of change which will be familiar to students of the history of other parts of the Mediterranean world in the sixteenth, seventeenth, and eighteenth centuries. Throughout this area, as Fernand Braudel has shown for the latter sixteenth century, the old bourgeoisie, so active and vital in earlier times, tended to dissolve. The wealthier families were transformed into a landed aristocracy, while others merged with the lower classes. Particularly where the economy was stagnant, as in much of Italy, the replenishment of the middle class was so slow and

126

quantitatively so insufficient that the group lost much of its social individuality.[1] This study should contribute to the picture of the Venetian aspects of this general change which has been emerging from the studies of Beltrami and others.[2] In Venice the " failure of the bourgeoisie" took place in two ways. First, the nobility—originally composed essentially of merchants—adopted more aristocratic customs. With their overseas commerce in decline, the nobles gradually withdrew from trade. Perhaps modelling themselves on other nobilities, the Venetian patricians then began to buy land and build villas and to look on their former way of life with contempt. By the middle of the seventeenth century they could speak of admitting new merchant families to the nobility as " prostituting " an " unstained Virgin." Thus the leading Venetian merchants of the medieval and Renaissance period were transformed from merchant patricians into land-owning aristocrats. Then, the Venetian middle class continued to dwindle in the seventeenth and eighteenth centuries when many of the still active merchants and manufacturers of the city and its environs bought their way into the nobility. Once admitted, they were glad to adopt patrician airs themselves and to give up trade and industry.

Thus Venice made a transformation common to many cities in Italy, Spain, and elsewhere in the Mediterranean area. " Modern " cities have populations active in industry, trade, or administration. But Venice and others like her in southern Europe became centers in which groups of wealthy nobles were surrounded by constellations of lesser nobles, lawyers, priests, shopkeepers, tailors, entertainers, and servants, dependent for their living on the patronage of a few wealthy aristocrats. There were to be important implications for the nineteenth century unification movement in the lack of vigorous merchants and industrialists in many Italian cities, and in the dependence of the majority of

[1] For a general discussion see Fernand Braudel, *La Méditerranée et le Monde méditerranéen à l'époque de Philippe II* (Paris: Colin, 1949), pp. 616-62. For a few pages on Italy in particular, where the subject has received little attention, see Giorgio Candeloro, *Storia dell'Italia moderna: I Le origini del Risorgimento* (Milan: Feltrinelli, 1959), pp. 52-55.
[2] Daniele Beltrami, *Saggio di storia dell'agricoltura nella repubblica di Venezia durante l'età moderna* (Venice and Rome: Istituto per la Collaborazione Culturale, 1956) and *Storia della popolazione di Venezia.*

city-dwellers on the patronage of a small and conservative group of land-owners.

But it was not only the merchant class of Venice which dwindled. This study has been concerned much more with the decline in number of the nobility considered *as a ruling class*. Such decreases seem to have been common among many European upper class groups in the seventeenth and eighteenth centuries. Of the forty-five peerages created in England by Queen Anne, thirteen had become extinct before 1784.[3] Among the Spanish grandees in this period there was " an unusually frequent failure of male heirs, attributed by foreigners to aristocratic degeneracy." [4] Late marriages, celibacy, family limitation practices, and perhaps other factors caused the nineteen prominent Genevan families studied by Louis Henry to diminish after about 1700,[5] and a group of Swedish noble families studied by Fahlbeck declined in number in the seventeenth and eighteenth centuries for approximately the same reasons.[6] Probably there was a similar tendency among the upper classes all over Europe, but this would only be very evident where the families concerned were especially visible as members of ruling groups and where new families could not in some way join them. If there was such a general decline in the privileged groups, historians have commented on it rarely and studied it even less. Yet a decline in the number of men in these groups may have been important in bolstering aristocratic conservatism and provoking the opposed " democratic revolution " of the late eighteenth century. As families declined in size, they would have been better able to hold on to their wealth and social positions. Where families died out and were not replaced, those who remained would have appeared more oligarchic than when their class had been more numerous.

The exclusive character of the Venetian nobility makes its decline in number especially interesting from the standpoint of political theory. In *The Ruling Class*,[7] Gaetano Mosca distin-

[3] H. J. Habakkuk, " England," (Goodwin, *European nobility*, pp. 1-21), p. 17.
[4] Raymond Carr, " Spain," (Goodwin, *European nobility*, pp. 43-59), p. 49.
[5] Henry, *Anciennes familles*, 179.
[6] Pontus E. Fahlbeck, " La noblesse de Suède. Étude démographique," *Bulletin de l'Institut international de statistique*, XII (1900), No. 1, pp. 169-81.
[7] *The Ruling Class* (*Elementi di scienza politica*), Hannah D. Kahn, trans., ed., and rev. by Arthur Livingston, (New York and London: McGraw-Hill, 1939).

guishes between " democratic " and " aristocratic " ruling groups. As these words are used by the Italian political scientist, a " democratic " ruling group is one which occasionally admits new families, establishing mechanisms for this purpose, while an " aristocratic " class has no method of self-replenishment. The English aristocracy, with its gentry group open to anyone who could buy enough land, and even its peerage open in each century to a few families of wealth and political importance was and today is in Mosca's terminology, a " democratic " ruling class. More often it has been described as " flexible." The Venetian nobility, on the other hand, accepted virtually no families between 1380 and 1645, and in this period only those families left the nobility which died out. It thus becomes perhaps the classic example in European history of a closed, " aristocratic " ruling class. This study has shown what became of this closed nobility. When two severe plagues had taken their toll, when the custom of restricted marriages had begun to reduce the number of children born in each generation, when ways to acquire money decreased and ways to spend it remained constant, the capacity of this ruling class for its task lessened. No longer could it provide enough wealthy and qualified men for the offices of the Republic. Thus the Venetian experience becomes a fairly clear demonstration of the infeasibility in the long run of an " aristocratic " or closed ruling class. It is hardly a rigidly controlled, laboratory demonstration of this point, but it is as good an example as history can offer.

A GENERAL SURVEY OF THE SOURCES

This study is based on a wide variety of published sources and manuscripts. Here I mean to discuss only the archival series and some of the other manuscripts used at various points in my investigation. All of these are in the Archivio di Stato di Venezia, the Biblioteca Marciana, and the Biblioteca del Museo Correr. The latest and best guide to the archival sources is Andrea da Mosto, *L'Archivio di Stato di Venezia, indice generale, storico, descrittivo ed analitico, Tomo I, Archivi dell'amministrazione centrale della Repubblica Veneta e archivi notarili,* which was published in 1937.[1] Almost seventy years older, but a useful supplement to da Mosto's guide is Armand Baschet's *Les Archives de Venise.*[2] Heinrich Kretschmayr lists and comments briefly on a great many Venetian chronicles, diaries, political treatises, Venetian official histories, and the like in the back of each volume of his *Geschichte von Venedig.*[3]

In showing that some nobles dissipated their fortunes in spendthrift living, and in dealing with the problem of finding men for offices, sumptuary legislation and laws dealing with elections were particularly important sources. Most of the laws on these two subjects are in the series called *Senato Terra* and *Deliberazioni del Maggior Consiglio,* but for the period after 1500 alone, these comprise about 400 volumes, and it would have been a nearly hopeless task to work through them. Fortunately, I was able to use collections of sumptuary and election laws which are in the *Compilazione Leggi* of the Archivio di Stato. This is a compilation of decrees, decisions, reports, and laws on a great number of topics, which was made by a government official and some assistants in the eighteenth century in preparation for a codification of the laws which was never carried out. The compilers surveyed all Venetian legislation and copied and assembled by subject whatever seemed important.[4] Nat-

---

[1] Bibliothèque des " Annales Institutorum," Vol. V.

[2] *Les archives de Venise: Histoire de la chancellerie secrète, le sénat, le cabinet des ministres, le conseil des dix et les inquisiteurs d'état dans leurs rapports avec la France* (Paris: Plon, 1870).

[3] It was published in three volumes: Vol. I (Gotha: Perthes, 1905); Vol. II (Gotha: Perthes, 1920); Vol. III (Stuttgart: Perthes, 1934).

[4] See da Mosto, *L'Archivio di Stato,* I, pp. 80-81.

urally they left out a great deal and included particularly the more recent legislation. The material compiled on any one subject is never sufficient for a study on that topic, but since many laws refer back to earlier ones, the *Compilazione Leggi* is often a convenient starting point.

Buste [5] 197 through 202 in this compilation contain several hundred laws, reports, and decisions by the *Collegio* regarding elections to all kinds of offices, and *buste* 241 and 348 include much legislation on the Great Council and Senate elections respectively. These collections guided part of my investigation of the lack of candidates for offices. In studying the same subject, I also used the government's records of office-holders, which are contained in the 220 items of the series called *Segretario alle Voci*. The Archivio di Stato and the Marciana library possess lists of men who competed for offices between about 1500 and 1797. Each volume covers a period of five years.

For sumptuary legislation, I used *Compilazione Leggi, busta* 305, which is a rich collection of copies of such laws, dating back to 1299, as well as lists of many other decrees not copied, and reports of officials in charge of suggesting and enforcing sumptuary legislation. There are also many copies and summaries of them in *buste* 8 and 21 of the papers of the *Provveditori sopra le Pompe*. They seem to have been compiled in the seventeenth and eighteenth centuries.

The principal sources for the number of adult noblemen are discussed in Critical Note 2. In the course of studying the reasons for the decline in number, I looked at wills dating from the fifteenth through the eighteenth centuries. These are among the papers of the *Cancelleria Inferiore* and the *Archivio Notarile* (in the Archivio di Stato). The wills in these two collections date from about 1300 to 1850. (Many medieval wills are among the papers of the *procuratori di San Marco,* who were often made executors.) Each Venetian notary was required to make two "original" copies of a will and deposit one with the government. For most notaries there are *protocolli* or volumes of copies on parchment of all the wills they drew up. Because some notaries habitually drew up wills for nobles, a number of these *protocolli* had the advantage, for me, of grouping together many patrician wills of a particular period. Compared with the originals, they proved to be accurate copies, and they are usually more legible. Consequently, I used *protocolli* almost exclusively, being sure to examine the wills of both rich and poor noblemen.

The Barbaro genealogies provided a very useful complement to the wills.[6] These genealogies contain hundreds upon hundreds of family trees which the patrician Marco Barbaro first wrote down in the sixteenth cen-

---

[5] In the Italian archives, a *busta* is a thick folder containing documents.
[6] Cited, p. 61, n. 30.

tury and which other devoted genealogists continued until almost the end of the eighteenth century. They contain not only names and relationships of all male nobles but also years of birth, marriage, and death, names of wives, principal offices held and anything else the genealogists felt was of interest. The information is not always complete even in the later centuries, but when confronted with official records it usually proves to be accurate. Many old collections of genealogies of noble families are notoriously untrustworthy, but *Il Barbaro* is a comparatively solid and dependable work. Like the wills, these genealogies can be a very interesting and valuable source of information not only about specific individuals and families but about the customs of the nobility as a class.

For the speeches made in 1645 on the subject of accepting new families in the nobility, I used and have cited the printed version of Marcello's speech in Nani's official history and a copy of the Michiel speech in the Correr library's manuscript P.D. 96c. Both of these speeches can be found in several handwritten copies in the family archives which have been turned over to the Marciana and Correr libraries.[7] Those which I have consulted do not differ one from another, however, and I cited those mentioned above because they were respectively the most accessible and the most legible copies. The Great Council deliberations confirm that these two men did speak for and against the proposal to accept five new families into the nobility, but the texts may well contain embellishments made by these noblemen or others after the speeches had been delivered. I have found no manuscript copies of the speech made by Foscarini in 1684, and the version of this speech which Foscarini himself reports in his own history of the latter part of the seventeenth century differs somewhat from the paraphrase reported by Garzoni in his still later official history. The principal source for the speeches made concerning the proposal in 1774 and 1775 to accept more new families is Balbi's *Relazione delle cose.* (For the citation, see Chapter II, fn. 49.) The copy I used is found among the manuscripts left by the nineteenth-century Venetian historian, Emmanuele Cicogna. In the catalogue of his collection, Cicogna says that he bought this manuscript from the author's heirs. If Balbi had any strong feelings for or against the proposal to accept new families, it is not evident in his report of the discussions in the Great Council.

There are two principal sources of information about the kinds of families who were ennobled between 1646 and 1718. One is the requests which the families themselves made for the status of nobility. In these they mentioned past services rendered to the Republic and tried to de-

---

[7] Both speeches are contained in Correr, P.D. 96c; Correr, Grad. 84; Marc., It. VII, 2487 (10547); and Correr, Donà 474.

scribe themselves as the kind of people who would make good Venetian nobles. Generally these requests give only a pale and indistinct picture of their authors. There is more information in the handwritten books of descriptions of these families which abound in the archives and libraries of Venice. From their scorn for many of the new families, I would guess that these were composed by old family nobles. They differ from each other to a greater or lesser extent, but all contain a paragraph on each new family that tells whether the men ennobled were mainland nobles, *cittadini,* or merchants, where they came from, a few other particulars, and the votes which they received in the Senate and Great Council. I used the Archivio di Stato's Miscellanea Codici 760 and 866 because of their availability and legibility, and because they complement each other well; and the Correr's Gradenigo 32 because it contains a few notes concerning the fate of the families after they entered the nobility.

CRITICAL NOTE 2

SOURCES FOR THE NUMBER OF VENETIAN NOBLES DURING
THE LAST THREE CENTURIES OF THE REPUBLIC

The sources for the number of nobles during the first two-thirds of the sixteenth century are difficult to use and can give only approximate totals. The information which I used in arriving at the numbers presented in Chapter III is contained in this table:

Year	Number of Men	Who are Comprised in This Number	Source
1493	2,600	(The figure is preceded by a discussion of the admission by lot of men under twenty-five.) Sanuto says " si ritrovano esser patritij 2600 in tutto, de li quali molti n'è fuori in rezimenti, viazi et mesi, et altri che non continua li consegii . . ."	Marino Sanuto, *Cronachetta,* Venice: Visentini, 1880, pp. 221-22.
1513	2,662	A list of families with the number of men in each who " mettono ballotti in Gran Cons°.," or " se attrovan provadi nel mazor Cons°."	Marc., It. VII, 90 (8029), pp. 349-50.
1527	2,705	" Queste sono tutte le caxade de zentilhomeni vivi, ne l'anno 1527 a dì 30 Luio." A list like that of 1513.	Sanuto, *Diarii,* XLV, col. 569-72.

Year	Number of Men	Who are Comprised in This Number	Source
1550	2,615	A book listing names of men, but no birth dates or fathers' names, entitled "Notatorio de'tutti zentilhomeni vengono à gran conseglio l'anno 1550." I have determined that some of the men were under twenty-five years old.	Marc., It. VII, 154 (8866).
1563	2,435	"Nobili-Homini," excluding "putti" 17 and under. A census. Presumably nobles away from Venice at the time were not counted.	Correr, Donà 53, p. 157.

There is no problem in understanding what age group was included in the 1563 census figures. But the words used in connection with the figures for 1493, 1513, 1527, and 1550 do not make it clear whether these cover (1) All noblemen aged twenty-five or more, or (2) Those aged twenty-five or more plus those aged twenty to twenty-four who had been admitted to the Great Council by lot. It might be, of course, that each of the figures for the four years has a different coverage. However, they do not diverge very much from one another and, in rising from 2,662 (in 1513) to 2,705 (in 1527) they indicate an increase in the number of noblemen which is mentioned in the preambles to two laws passed in the 1520's (see discussion in Chapter III). Furthermore, the lists which the figures for 1513 and 1527 come from are very similar in the way they were drawn up, and the phrases used with the figures for 1513 and 1550 are similar. Therefore, I believe that all four of these figures cover either one or the other of the two groups mentioned above.

In no cases do the phrases used with these figures exclude the possibility that those admitted by lot to the Great Council were included in the total, and in the case of the figure for 1493, I believe that the younger men were included because, just before giving the number, Sanuto mentions the number of these younger men who entered the Great Council by lot each year. I am also sure that the younger men were included in the list for 1550 because I have discovered by checking their names with official records that at least some of the men in this list were less than twenty-five years old. Because, as I explained above, all four figures seem to have the same coverage, it is probable that if two of them refer to all men aged twenty-five or more, plus the younger men who had been admitted by lot, then all four figures cover this group. It is not clear to me just how it would have been possible in those years to determine exactly how many men were entitled to be in the Great Council. But the major problem would have been to draw up the first list of all the noblemen in the Great Council, including the men who had been admitted by lot. (It may be that such lists had been made for a long time before the sixteenth century, but none seem to have survived.) Once a list had been drawn up, it would have been possible gradually to correct it and keep it up-to-date by adding the names of young men as they entered the Great Council—by lot or at the age of twenty-five—and by removing the names of those who died. No official list of those who entered each year survives, but the Marciana library possesses a manuscript which records the names of all nobles who entered the Great Council each year between 1520 and 1580, and no doubt the government or private individuals kept many such lists.[1] Naturally the records of births kept by the government —in the *Libri d'Oro*—would be of little help since many boys would have died between birth and the age of twenty-five. (These records may have been consulted by the compilers for birth dates and fathers' names.) To learn who were removed from the Great Council by death, a compiler of a list of members could have consulted records kept by the *Avogaria del Comun* and by private individuals.[2]

If these figures then include not only the men aged twenty-five or more, but also those between twenty and twenty-four who were admitted by lot to the Great Council, the next problem is to learn how many were admitted by lot and subtract their number from the total. (This study is concerned only with men over twenty-five who could hold offices.) Sanuto indicates that in 1493 roughly sixty men under twenty-five were entering the Great Council annually. (His meaning is somewhat obscure and the number may have been higher.) If this had been happening over a five-year period, and if we assume that twelve of the sixty men were aged twenty, that twelve were twenty-one years old and so on, then in 1493 the under twenty-five group would number about 180. Subtracting this from 2,600, I conclude that in 1493 there were about 2,420 noblemen aged twenty-five or more. The system for admitting by lot seems to have changed in the following decades, because Giannotti says that a maximum of thirty-one were admitted each year at the time he wrote.[3] I am inclined to believe that this would have been true of all the other three figures. On that basis one should subtract about ninety from each of them, and I have done this. It appears that the men aged twenty-five or more numbered very roughly 2,420 in 1493, 2,570 in 1513, 2,620 in 1527, and 2,520 in 1550.

---

[1] Marc., It. VII, 362 (7933).
[2] A.S.V., Avogaria del comun, b. 159.
[3] Donato Giannotti, *Libro de la repubblica de' Vinitiani* (Rome: Blado, 1542), p. 16v.

Beginning in 1594, it is possible to obtain fairly accurate figures on the numbers of noblemen from *libri di nobili* (books of noblemen) which were compiled frequently after that time and which list all noblemen aged eighteen or more at the time of compilation, with birth dates and fathers' names. It may be that the lists of families and the number in each family for 1513 and 1527 were drawn from such books. The *libro di nobili* for 1550, in contrast to those earlier lists, is in book form and gives the names of all the men in each family. But it does not provide fathers' names or birth dates, and the latter are indispensable for eliminating the under twenty-five men from the total. A *libro di nobili* for 1594 (Correr, Donà 225) is the first to provide birth dates.

Presumably what was said about the formation of the lists of families in 1513 and 1527 applies also to the way the *libri di nobili* were composed. The same kinds of information could have been used. In Venice there are a number of published and handwritten lists of the young men who entered the Great Council each year and of those who died.[4]

Most of the *libri di nobili* probably belonged to patricians who were curious about the number of men in the different families or who wished to have at their fingertips the names of men who might be elected to different posts as they became vacant. Among some eighteenth century papers of the Donà family are lists of men who were at the time serving in governorships, holding other key offices, or not interested in serving in the government. Perhaps a *libro di nobili* was put to use in drawing up these lists.

The main problem involved in using these books to learn the number of noblemen aged twenty-five or more in a given year arises from the fact that the books also list men under twenty-five. Probably these were men admitted to the Great Council by lot before they reached the age at which all noblemen automatically became members. In order to eliminate them from my count, I had to find in what year the book was compiled and then count only those men whose birth dates indicated that they were at least twenty-five. In other words, if I had a book composed on August 1, 1650, I counted only men who had been born before August 1, 1625. The figures derived may not be perfectly accurate. This should be clear from the doubts expressed above regarding how a compiler could have known with much certainty who had just entered the

---

[4] On the noblemen who annually entered the Great Council, see, in addition to Marc., It. VII, 362 (7993), which has already been cited, V. M. Coronelli, *Cronologia dei veneti patrizi,* Venice, 1714. (Cited in Beltrami, *Storia della popolazione,* p. 75.) On the annual number of deaths see A.S.V., Avogaria de comun, b. 159; an unnumbered book of nobles dead between 1687-1768 in A.S.V., Segretario alle voci; and Marc., It. VII, 353 (7931).

Great Council or who had died in recent months. Perhaps the margin of the compiler's error would be as much as twenty or thirty.

There are a great number of these books of noblemen's names in the *Archivio di Stato* and the libraries of Venice. I have cited some of them in Chapter III, but it may be useful to list here all those already mentioned, and others spaced out at approximately five-year intervals. In those cases where I have counted the noblemen over twenty-four, I have put the total in the column in the middle: [5]

Year in Which Compiled	No. of Noblemen Aged Twenty-five and Over	Location
1550	2,615	Marc., It. VII, 154 (8866).
1594	1,970	Correr, Donà 225.
1609	2,090	Correr, P.D. 368b.
1620	2,000	Correr, Cic. 37.
1631	1,660	Correr, Cic. 18.
1637	1,675	Correr, P.D. 367b.
1652	1,540	Correr, Cic. 9.
1656	—	Correr, Cic. 140.
1661	—	Correr, Cor. 3.
1664	—	Marc., It. VII, 183 (8161), fols. 291-321
1671	1,590	Correr, Cic. 16.
1677	—	Correr, Cic. 918.
1683	1,560	Marc., It. VII, 1259 (7537).
1686	1,605	Correr, Cic. 919.
1691	—	Correr, Grad. 10.
1697	—	Correr, P.D. 60b.
1703	—	Correr, Cor. 93.
1710	—	Correr, P.D. 43a.
1715	1,750	Correr, Cor. 94.
1719	1,710	Correr, P.D. 5b.
1726	1,640	Marc. It. VII, 2163 (7380).

For the period from 1726 to 1760, few if any *libri di nobili* are to be found. For the years from 1760 to 1797, the almanacs which are cited in Chap. III, fn. 65 contain what are equivalent to *libri di nobili*. They provided totals of 1,300 men in 1775 and 1,090 in 1797.

I did not make use of censuses, which are the other major source of

[5] These figures have been rounded off to the nearest number divisible by five to emphasize that there may have been small errors in the counting.

information on the number of noblemen. Censuses were made in Venice as early as 1338, but only by the sixteenth century do they supply numbers of nobles. After the middle of this century, the information was collected by parish priests, who made door-to-door checks and wrote the required information on carefully prepared, printed forms.[6] There are many problems connected with the census figures for the sixteenth century. For 1509 the figures are complete for only three of the six major divisions of the city; the transcriber of the results of another census wrote down totals which are so different from the correct totals of his figures that it appears that he must have confused two different censuses. The population figures in another census are so out of proportion with other roughly contemporary figures as to make them incredible.[7]

The censuses for the seventeenth and eighteenth centuries are good for their time, but I preferred to use the *libri di nobili*. These were my reasons:

1. The census figures for nobles in the sixteenth century are questionable for the reasons explained above.

2. The *libri di nobili* seem to be based on carefully kept government records, or lists derived therefrom, and apparently they include all Venetian noblemen living in a given year. It appears that the priests who took the censuses counted only noblemen living in Venice at the time the count was made.

3. With the *libri di nobili* it is possible to obtain the number of men aged twenty-five or over, and this is the significant figure for the purposes of this study. The censuses, on the other hand, offer totals of noblemen aged eighteen or more residing in Venice at the time the count was made. This number was less useful to me.

---

[6] For an example of one of these forms, see Correr, Donà 351.

[7] See Aldo Contento, " Il censimento della popolazione sotto la repubblica veneta," *Archivio Veneto*, 1900, XIX: pt. I, pp. 5-42; pt. II, pp. 179-240; and XX: pt. I, pp. 5-96; pt. II, pp. 171-223. Also Julius Beloch, " La popolazione di Venezia nei secoli xvi e xvii," *Nuovo Archivio Veneto*, Vol. III (1902), pt. I.

CRITICAL NOTE 3

VENETIAN POLITICAL OBSERVERS OF THE SEVENTEENTH AND EIGHTEENTH CENTURIES

Venice produced few important political thinkers—none to compare, for example, with Botero, Montesquieu, or Burke. This may have been the result of government censorship. Books printed in the Republic had to be approved by a commission of noblemen, and probably most of these men did not have a taste for thought-provoking political writing. The sixteenth century treatises of Contarini and Paruta are bland, and the official Venetian histories testify to the government's conservatism. But the very smoothness with which the Venetian government ran may have been just as responsible for the lack of original political thought. The constitution evolved slowly; there were no dramatic changes to call attention to political alternatives. True, some noblemen could see the systems of other countries in their capacities as ambassadors, and these men wrote reports which are models of keen and interesting observation. But the ambassadors were principal members of the ruling group and they were not stimulated by their foreign experiences to challenge the basis of their own government.

Some Venetians, however, did write essays and books about their government during the last two centuries of the Republic, and these have been of some use in this study. Most of them were written by noblemen who were not important members of the government. None of them attack the aristocratic constitution itself, but in general they are marked by resentment against the *grandi* and it is significant that none of them were published before the fall of the Republic. I have written these notes on the books because I have used them in this study, and because most of them are not well-known even to Venetian historians.

1. Anonymous, *Esame Istorico Politico di cento soggetti della repubblica veneta* (1675).[1] The author of this unpublished book explains his purpose in the opening paragraphs of his work. He aims to assay the merits of 100 leading Venetians the same way that a government mintmaster measures the gold in a coin newly issued by another state, to learn if it has the value it purports to have. He will discuss the abilities of these noblemen and their foreign policy preferences in a manner which may often be harsh, but will also be truthful. After an introductory general discussion of the ruling class, he provides one hundred

---

[1] Correr, Grad. 15.

witty and interesting sketches of leading senators, sketches which are often quite specific about the wealth, family, and political career, and the private interests, abilities, and foreign policy leanings of his subjects.

On the whole, the writer seems to have lived up to his promise to be truthful. While his judgments are frequently severe they have an honest ring. One might expect this to be a political pamphlet directed against some group of nobles, but his portraits do not bear this out. He reports policy preferences with no hint that his judgments are based on them. Where he despises a noble it is because of the man's incapacity or laziness. Because of the writer's apparently intimate knowledge of Venetian political matters and personalities, I suspect that he was a nobleman.

I have used the *Esame Istorico Politico* principally for the writer's general remarks about the wealth of the nobility, undesired government offices, the maturity of senators and ambassadors, and the ladders of offices which were to be found in the Venetian political system. There is no reason to suspect that political prejudices affected what he had to say on these subjects.

2. Anonymous, *Relazione del anonimo,* apparently written between 1659 and 1665.[2] This is another collection of sketches of Venetian noblemen so like the *Esame Istorico Politico* that I suspect that the same person wrote both works. Pompeo Molmenti discovered the manuscript in the archives of Turin and published it in 1919. I used it principally for what it has to say about the wealth of old and new families.

3. Giannantonio Muazzo, *Del Governo Antico della repubblica veneta, delle alterazioni, e regolazioni d'esso, e delle Cause, e tempi, che sono successe fino a nostri giorni: discorso istorico politico,* MS, written 1670-1699,[3] and *Storia del governo antico e presente della Repubblica di Venezia,* MS, written in the latter half of the seventeenth century.[4] Muazzo was a Venetian nobleman whose family, like a considerable number of others, lived on the island of Crete until the Venetian-Turkish war over the island in the mid-seventeenth century. Then in his late twenties, Muazzo fought bravely in this war as a ship captain. But the Republic lost Crete, and Muazzo went to live in Venice along with numerous other impoverished noble families. Evidently he was not so poor as the others since he is said to have owned a large library of manuscripts and printed books. He served in the government, but was primarily a scholar who wrote a number of historical works — as yet all unpublished — on

---

[2] *Relazione del anonimo,* in Pompeo Molmenti, *Curiosità di Storia Veneziana* (Bologna: Zanichelli, 1919), pp. 359-438.

[3] Marc., It. VII, 964 (7831). (Also Correr, Cic. 2000.)

[4] Marc., It. VII, 966 (8406).

the history of Crete, the noble families who had lived there, the recently-ended war, and the Venetian constitution.[5]

To judge from internal evidence, Muazzo wrote *Del Governo Antico* over a period of three decades.[6] It deals with the office of the doge, the origins and *serrata* (or closing) of the Great Council, the number of men in this body at different times, and the reasons for its decrease in size; how elections were held in Venice, and the relative authority of the Great Council, Senate and *Quarantia*. Muazzo was well-informed, and he has thoughtful things to say about the *serrata* and the nature of the nobility. An example of his ingenuity: he went to the trouble of finding out how many noblemen had, over the previous two centuries, voted in the always hotly contested elections of procurators; in this way he demonstrated quite clearly that the nobility had diminished. Evidently not a member of the core of the ruling group, he nevertheless had no great prejudice against the *grandi*. The fact that *Del Governo Antico* was never published is probably explained by the candor with which Muazzo discusses such matters as the *serrata,* the decline in number of the nobility, and the conflict of powers between the Senate and Great Council. I have made use of what he has to say on the decrease of the nobility, a plan to accept new families, and the ladders of offices.

The *Storia del governo* is less interesting than *Del Governo Antico*. It consists partly of constitutional history, and partly of description of the government of Venice in the seventeenth century. I used this source for Muazzo's remarks about refusals of offices and the fact that poorer noblemen relied on the lesser offices for their livelihood.

4. Anonymous, *Relazione Della Serenissima Repubblica di Venezia, con la quale si descrivono i modi del suo Governo, i mezzi per tener a freno la Nobiltà; Le Massime de Privati: La Politica che addopra con i Sudditi; Il genio e le preteze co' Prencipi; Le sue forze ordinarie con che possa operare in un straordinario Armamento; L'abbondanza del Dinaro e la sicurezza, o il dubbio alla permanenza. Scritta dal NU Senator* [crossed out and replaced with:] *Ambasciator dalla Torre Cesareo Del 1682*. This manuscript of the Marciana library [7] appears to have been written by a Venetian nobleman near the end of the seventeenth century. The writer says that he served for forty years in the Senate, twenty of them in the *Collegio,* and implies that he had often served as ambassa-

---

[5] The preceding information about Muazzo comes from Emanuele Antonio Cicogna, *Delle iscrizioni veneziane* (6 vols..; Venice [various publishers], 1824-1853), III, 390-94.

[6] Cicogna remarks that Muazzo's literary style is not to be despised, "considering the unfortunate century" in which it was written.

[7] Marc., It. VII, 1533 (8826).

dor or governor.[8] In a printed version of a variant copy of the *Relazione* which appeared in 1846,[9] the author does not mention government service, but does speak of his love for Venice. It appears, therefore, that a Venetian, probably a nobleman, was the author of this *Relazione*. However, someone has crossed out the words *NU Senator* on the title page of the manuscript and replaced them with the name of a late seventeenth century Austrian ambassador to Venice. My guess is that this person had confused this *Relazione* with another with a similar name by the Austrian ambassador.[10]

The long title gives a general idea of the contents of this work. The author's main preoccupation is with the *grandi* and their abuses of power, their struggles against the virtuous nobles of moderate means who strive merely to provide good government, and their corruption of the poor nobles. He fears that the *grandi* will soon cause the downfall of the Republic. But he concentrates on the evils of the rule of the *grandi*, while accepting the fact of their holding of offices. He does not accuse them of trying to monopolize key offices (except for a very few lucrative ones). Therefore his work, unlike that of Curti which I will discuss below, is not a challenge to my thesis (expressed in Chapter IV) that there were ever fewer men able and willing to fill the highest offices. In any case, his acrimony, his occasional unfairness, and his obsession with injustices committed by the *grandi* lessen one's confidence in what he has to say about them. I have made use principally of what this anonymous author has to say regarding the *grandi,* the wealth and education of the nobility, a plan to accept new families, and the ladders of offices. I have quoted from the Marciana's manuscript, rather than the printed and slightly different version, which came to my attention later.

5. Leopoldo Curti, *Memorie istoriche e politiche sopra la Repubblica di Venezia, scritte l'anno 1792 da Leopoldo Curti.*[11] Curti belonged to a " new " family ennobled in 1680. While serving as governor of Vicenza, he seems to have been accused of " abuse of power," and investigated by the inquisitors of state. In any case, he left Venice under a cloud and

---

[8] P. 137.

[9] Giuseppe Bacco (ed.), *Relazione sulla organizzazione politica della Repubblica di Venezia al cadere del secolo decimosettimo . . . manoscritto inedita di un contemporaneo . . .* (Vicenza: Picutti, 1846).

[10] Cicogna (*Delle iscrizioni veneziane*, 1, 41) discussses the ambassador dalla Torre and his *Relazione o sia esame della Repubb. di Venezia*. Later, (IV, 676) he states that the dalla Torre work was a plagiarism from Abraham-Nicolas Amelot de la Houssaie, *Histoire du gouvernement de Venise*. The Marciana *Relazione* has no resemblance to Amelot de la Houssaie's book.

[11] Venice: Parolaris, 1812.

without permission to depart.[12] He went to St. Petersburg, later perhaps to London, and then to Switzerland, where in 1792 he wrote his book about the Venetian government. The first part of this work merely describes the organization and functioning of the Venetian constitution. Part II bitterly criticizes the old, rich families (the *grandi*) who, he claims, monopolized all positions as *savi grandi* and as members of the Council of Ten. He is particularly bitter against the three inquisitors of state (two of whom were always chosen for the Council of Ten) and claims that these men perpetually tried to create discord the better to manage the state.[13] Curti was not the first to attack the *grandi*, as I have shown, but he is the only Venetian whose writings I have come upon who, during the time of the Republic, accused the *grandi* of monopolizing offices and consciously excluding nobles not in their group. It may be that his animus reflects not only his own personality, his experience with the inquisitors, and resentment of his position as a " new " family noble, but also the influence of the French Revolution. I have used his comments on the *grandi* and his estimate of the numbers of nobles who were poor, wealthy, and of moderate means during the last years of the Republic.

6. Giovanni Pindemonte, untitled essay on the decadence of the Venetian government, written in 1796.[14] For a discussion of this nobleman see the latter part of Chapter V. Pindemonte wrote his treatise with the expressed aim of describing the decadence of the Venetian government. As with Curti's book, this one should be used with a certain amount of caution. Pindemonte too belonged to a " new " family, had had difficulties with the government, and wrote in the time of the French Revolution. I have made use of what he has to say on the declining number of old families and their continual service as *savi grandi*, and of his description of the senators happily rushing out of a session like boys out of school.

---

[12] See A.S.V., Inquisitori di stato, b. 909, report of 1 Oct. 1789, paragraph 11; and b. 1148.

[13] Pt. II, pp. 67-70, 153, 230.

[14] The essay is in Giuseppe Biadego (ed.), *Poesie e lettere di Giovanni Pindemonte* (Bologna: Zanichelli, 1883), Appendix I, pp. 325-50.

PUBLISHED BOOKS AND ARTICLES
CITED IN THIS STUDY

Amelot de la Houssaie, Abraham-Nicolas, *Histoire du gouvernement de Venise.* Paris: Leonard, 1677.

Bacco, Giuseppe (ed.), *Relazione sulla organizzazione politica della Repubblica di Venezia al cadere del secolo decimosettimo . . . manoscritto inedito di un contemporaneo.* Vicenza: Picutti, 1856.

Barozzi, Nicolo and Berchet, Guglielmo (eds.), *Le relazioni degli stati europei lette al Senato dagli ambasciatori veneziani nel secolo decimosettimo.* 10 vols. Venice: Naratovich, 1856-1878.

Baschet, Armand, *Les archives de Venise: Histoire de la chancellerie secrète, le sénat, le cabinet des ministres, le conseil des dix et les inquisiteurs d'état dans leurs rapports avec la France.* Paris: Plon, 1870.

Battistella, Antonio, *La Repubblica di Venezia ne' suoi undici secoli di storia,* Venice: Ferrari, 1921.

Baur, Erwin; Fisher, Eugen; and Lenz, Fritz, *Menschliche Erblehre und Rassenhygiene.* 3rd ed. 2 vols. Munich: Lehmanns, 1936.

Beccaria, Cesare, *Elementi di economia pubblica di Cesar Beccaria milanese,* vols. 18 and 19 in *Scrittori classici italiani di economia politica,* 50 vols. Milan: Destefanis, 1803-16.

Beloch, Julius, " La popolazione di Venezia nei secoli xvi e xvii," *Nuovo Archivio Veneto* (n.s.), III (1902), pt. 1.

Beltrami, Daniele, *Saggio di storia dell'agricoltura nella repubblica di Venezia durante l'età moderna.* Venice and Rome: Istituto per la Collaborazione Culturale, 1956.

————, *Storia della popolazione di Venezia dalla fine del secolo xvi, alla caduta della Repubblica.* Padua. Cedam, 1954.

————, " Un ricordo del Priuli intorno al problema dell'ammortimento dei depositi in zecca, del 1574," in *Studi in onore di Armando Sapori,* 2 vols. Milan: Cisalpino, 1957.

Berengo, Andrea, *Lettres d'un marchand vénitien, Andrea Berengo (1553-1556).* Avant-propos de Gino Luzzatto, ed. Ugo Tucci. Paris: S.E.V.P.E.N., 1957.

Berengo, Marino, *La società veneta alla fine del settecento: ricerche storiche.* Florence: Sansoni, 1956.

Besta, Enrico, *Il Senato veneziano. Origini, attribuzioni, e riti.* Miscellanea, Series II, Vol. V. Venice: Deputazione (R.) veneta di Storia Patria, 1899.

Bilanci generali della repubblica di Venezia. 3 vols. Venice: R. Commissione dei documenti finanziarii della Repubblica di Venezia, 1903-1912.

Bistort, Giulio, *Il magistrato alle pompe nella repubblica di Venezia.* Miscellanea, Series III, Vol. V. Venice: Deputazione (R.) veneta di Storia Patria, 1912.

Bonetti, Bruno Brunelli, " Un riformatore mancato: Angelo Querini," *Archivio Veneto,* XLVIII-XLIX (1951), pp. 185-200.

144

Bratti, Riciotti, *I Codici Nobiliari del Museo Correr di Venezia.* Extract from *Rivista Araldica* (1907). Rome: Collegio Araldico, 1908.

Braudel, Fernand, *La Méditerranée et le monde méditerranéen à l'époque de Philippe II.* Paris: Colin, 1949.

———, "La vita economica di Venezia nel secolo XVI." *La civiltà veneziana del rinascimento.* Venice: Centro di cultura e civiltà della fondazione Giorgio Cini, 1958, pp. 81-102.

Brown, Horatio F., *The Venetian Printing Press: An Historical Study.* New York: Putnam's, 1891.

Brugi, Biagio, "Fedecommesso (Diritto romano, intermedio, odierno)." *Il digesto italiano: Enciclopedia metodica e alfabetica di legislazione, dottrina e giurisprudenza,* Vol. XI, Pt. I. Torino: Unione tipografico-editrice, 1884-1921, pp. 588-660.

Brunetti, Mario, "'Marin Sanudo' (profilo storico)," *Ateneo Veneto,* (1933), pp. 51-67.

Canal, Bernardo, "Il collegio, l'ufficio e l'archivio dei Dieci Savi alle Decime in Rialto," *Nuovo Archivio Veneto,* XVI (1908), pp. 115-50, 279-310.

Candeloro, Giorgio, *Storia dell'Italia moderna: I Le origini del Risorgimento.* Milan: Feltrinelli, 1959.

Cenni storici sopra la peste di Venezia del 1630-31 . . . (Author: "C.F."), Venice: Graziosi, 1830.

Cessi, Roberto (ed.), *Deliberazioni del maggior consiglio di Venezia.* 3 vols. Atti delle assemblee costituzionali italiane dal medio evo al 1831, serie terza: Parlamenti e consigli maggiori dei comuni italiani, sezione prima: Deliberazioni del maggior consiglio di Venezia. Rome: Accademia nazionale dei lincei; Commissione per gli atti delle assemblee costituzionali italiane, 1931-1950.

———, *Le origini del ducato veneziano.* Collana Storica, Vol. IV. Naples: Morano, 1951.

———, *Politica ed economia di Venezia nel trecento. Saggi.* Rome: Edizioni di "Storia e letteratura," 1952.

———, *Storia della repubblica di Venezia.* 2 vols. Milan-Messina: Principato, 1946.

Cicogna, Emmanuele Antonio, *Delle iscrizioni veneziane.* 6 vols. Venice: various publishers, 1824-1852.

Conigliani, Nerina, *Giovanni Sagredo.* Venice: Emiliana, 1934.

Contarini, Gasparo, *La Republica e i magistrati di Vinegia.* Venice: Sabini, 1551.

Contento, Aldo, "Il censimento della popolazione sotto la repubblica veneta," *Archivio Veneto,* Vol. XIX, pt. I, pp. 5-42, pt. II, pp. 179-240; Vol. XX, pt. I, pp. 5-96, pt. II, pp. 171-223.

Corti, Ugo, "La francazione del debito pubblico della repubblica di Venezia proposta da Gian Francesco Priuli," *Nuovo Archivio Veneto,* VII (1904), pp. 331-64.

Cozzi, Gaetano, *Il doge Nicolò Contarini. Ricerche sul patriziato veneziano agli inizi del Seicento.* Venice: Istituto per la collaborazione culturale, 1958.

Curti, Leopoldo, *Memorie istoriche e politiche sopra la Repubblica di Venezia scritte l'anno 1792 da Leopoldo Curti.* Venice: Parolaris, 1812.

Daru, Pierre A. N. B., *Histoire de la république de Venise.* 8 vols. Paris: Firmin Didot, 1821.

Degl'istorici delle cose veneziane, I quali hanno scritto per Pubblico Decreto (edn. of official Venetian histories). Battista Nani. *Historia della repubblica veneta.* 2 vols. Venice: Louisa, 1720; Michele Foscarini. *Historia della repubblica veneta.* Venice: Louisa, 1722; Pietro Garzoni. *Istoria della repubblica di Venezia.* 2 vols. Venice: Manfrè, 1719-1720.

Einaudi, Luigi. " L'economia pubblica veneziana dal 1736 al 1755," *La Riforma Sociale,* XIV (1904), pp. 177-96, 261-82, 429-50, 509-37.

Filangieri, Gaetano, *La Scienza della legislazione.* Venice: Santini, 1822.

Freschot, Casimir, *Nouvelle relation de la ville et république de Venise.* Utrecht: Poolsum, 1709.

Gallo, Rodolfo, " Una famiglia patrizia: I Pisani ed i palazzi di S. Stefano e di Strà," *Archivio Veneto,* XXXIV-XXXV (1944), pp. 65-228.

Giannotti, Donato, *Libro de la repubblica de' Vinitiani.* Rome: Blado, 1542.

Goodwin, A., (ed.) *The European Nobility in the Eighteenth Century: Studies of the Nobilities of the Major European States in the pre-Reform Era.* London: Black, 1953.

Gozzi, Gasparo, *Gazzetta veneta, di Gasparo Gozzi,* ed. Bruno Romani. Milan: Bompiani, 1943.

Guicciardini, Francesco, *Opere inedite di . . .; illustrate da Giuseppe Canestini e pubblicate per cura dei conti Pieri e Luigi Guicciardini.* 10 vols. in 5. Florence: Cellini, 1857-1867.

Henry, Louis, *Anciennes familles genevoises: Étude démographique: XVIᵉ-XXᵉ siècle.* Institut national d'études démographiques, Travaux et Documents, Cahier n⁰ 26, Presses universitaires de France, 1956.

Hodgson, Francis C., *Venice in the Thirteenth and Fourteenth Centuries—a Sketch of Venetian History from the Conquest of Constantinople to the Accession of Michele Steno. A.D. 1204-1400.* London: George Allen and Sons, 1910.

Kretschmayr, Heinrich, *Geschichte von Venedig.* 3 vols. I, Gotha: Perthes, 1905; II, Gotha: Perthes, 1920; III, Stuttgart: Perthes, 1934.

Lane, Frederic C., *Andrea Barbarigo: Merchant of Venice 1418-1449.* The Johns Hopkins University Studies in Historical and Political Science, Series LXII, No. 1. Baltimore: The Johns Hopkins Press, 1944.

————, " Family Partnerships and Joint Ventures in the Venetian Republic," *Journal of Economic History,* IV, No. 2 (1944) pp. 178-96.

————, " The Mediterranean Spice Trade (Further Evidence of its Revival in the Sixteenth Century)," *American Historical Review,* XLV (1940), pp. 581-90.

————, " National Wealth and Protection Costs," *War as a Social Institution,* ed. J. D. Clarkson and T. C. Cochran. New York: Columbia University Press, 1941.

————, " Venetian Shipping during the Commercial Revolution," *American Historical Review,* XXXVIII (1933), pp. 219-39.

Lazzarini, Vittorio, " Obbligo di assumere pubblici uffici nelle antiche leggi veneziane," *Archivio Veneto,* XIX (1936), pp. 184-91.

————, " Le offerte per la guerra di Chioggia e un falsario del quattrocento," *Nuovo Archivio Veneto* (n.s.), IV (1902), pp. 202-13.

Luzzatto, Gino, " La decadenza di Venezia dopo le scoperte geografiche nella tradizione e nella realtà," *Archivio Veneto,* LIV-LV (1954), pp. 162-81.

————, *Storia economica dell'età moderna e contemporanea.* Padua: Cedam, 1955.

————, *Studi di storia economica veneziana.* Padua: Milani, 1954.

Magalhães-Godinho, Vitorino, " Le repli vénitien et égyptien et la route du Cap 1496-1533." *Eventail de l'histoire vivante, hommage á Lucien Febvre . . .* 2 vols. Paris: Colin, 1953.

Maranini, Giuseppe, *La costituzione di Venezia dopo la serrata del maggior consiglio.* Venice, Perugia, Florence: La Nuova Italia, *ca.* 1931.

Marin, Carlo Antonio, *Storia civile e politica Del Commercio de'Veneziani,* 8 vols. Venice: Coleti, 1798-1808.

Memoria che può servir alla storia degli ultimi otto anni della Repubblica di Venezia, (anon.) London: Elvington, 1798.

Molmenti, Pompeo, *Curiosità di Storia Veneziana.* Bologna: Zanichelli, 1919. "Relazione di Monsr. Francesco Pannocchieschi," pp. 310-58; " Relazione del'anonimo," pp. 359 ff.

———, *La Storia di Venezia nella vita privata dalle origini alla caduta della Repubblica.* 8th ed., 3 vols. Bergamo: Istituto Italiano d'arti Grafiche, 1927.

Mosca, Gaetano, *The Ruling Class (Elementi di scienza politica).* Trans. by Hannah D. Kahn. Ed. and revis. with introd. by Arthur Livingston. New York and London: McGraw-Hill, 1939.

Mosto, Andrea da, *L'Archivio di Stato di Venezia, indice generale storico, descrittivo ed analitico.* Vol. I, *Archivi dell'amministrazione centrale della Repubblica Veneta e archivi notarili*; Vol. II, *Archivi dell'amministrazione provinciale della Repubblica Veneta, Archivi delle rappresentaze diplomatiche e consolari, Archivi dei governi succeduti alla repubblica veneta, Archivi degli istituti religiosi, e archivi minori,* in *Bibliothèque des " Annales Institutorum,"* Vol. 5, Rome, 1937-1940.

———, *I Dogi di Venezia con particolare riguardo alle loro tombe.* Venice: Ongania, n.d.

Mousnier, Roland, " Le trafic des offices à Venise." *Revue historique de droit français et étranger,* XXX (1952), pp. 552-65.

Muratori, Ludovico Antonio, *Dei difetti della giurisprudenza.* 2nd ed. Venice: Pasqualy, 1743.

Nani Mocenigo, Filippo, *Del dominio Napoleonico a Venezia (1806-1814) (note ed appunti).* Venice: Merlo, 1896.

New Cambridge Modern History, The. Vol. I, *The Renaissance 1493-1520,* ed. G. R. Potter. Cambridge: University Press, 1957.

Newett, Margaret, "The Sumptuary Laws of Venice in the Fourteenth and Fifteenth Centuries," in *Historical Essays by Members of the Owens College, Manchester,* ed. T. F. Tout and James Tait. London: Longmans, 1902, pp. 245-78.

Palmer, Robert R., *The Age of the Democratic Revolution: A Political History of Europe and America, 1760-1800,* Vol. I, *The challenge.* Princeton, N. J.: Princeton University Press, 1959.

Pastorello, Ester, *Tipografici, editori e librai a Venezia nel secolo xvi.* Florence: Olschki, 1924.

Pertile, Antonio, *Storia del diritto italiano dalla caduta dell'impero romano alla codificazione.* 6 vols., 2nd ed. Turin: Unione Tipografico-editrice, 1892-1898.

Petrocchi, Massimo, *Il tramonto della repubblica di Venezia e l'assolutismo illuminato.* Miscellanea. Vol. VII. Venice: Deputazione di storia per le Venezie, 1942.

Pindemonte, Giovanni, *Poesie e lettere di Giovanni Pindemonte,* ed. Giuseppe Biadego. Bologna: Zanichelli, 1883.

Ponte, Lorenzo Antonio da, *Osservazioni sopra li depositi nella Veneta zecca.* Venice, 1801.

Protogiornale per l'anno MDCCLIX [and succeeding years to 1797] *Ad uso della Serenissima Dominante Città di Venezia.* Venice: Bettinelli, 1759-1797.

Rodenwaldt, Ernst, " Pest in Venedig, 1575-1577. Ein Beitrag zur Frage der Infektikette bei den Pestepidemien West-Europas," *Sitsungsberichte der Heidelberger Akademie der Wissenschaften Mathematische-naturwissenschaftliche Klasse.* 1952, 2. Abhandlung.

————, "Untersuchungen über die Biologie des venezianischen Adels," *Homo,* VIII (1957), pp. 1-26.

Romanin, Samuele, *Storia documentata di Venezia.* 10 vols. Venice: Fuga, 1912-1921.

Rubin, Isidor C., "Sterility." *Encyclopaedia Britannica,* Vol. XXI. Chicago, Toronto, London, 1957, pp. 398-99.

Sandi, Vettore, *Principi di storia civile della repubblica di Venezia dalla sua fondazione sino all'anno di N.S. 1700.* 6 vols. Venice: Coleti, 1755.

————, *Principii di storia civile della repubblica di Venezia scritti da Vettor Sandi nobile veneto Dall'anno di N.S. 1700. sino all'anno 1767.* 3 vols. Venice: Coleti, 1772.

Sanuto, Marino, *Cronachetta di Marino Sanuto,* ed. Rinaldo Fulin. Venice: Visentini, 1880.

————, *I diarii.* 58 vols. Eds. Rinaldo Fulin, Nicolò Barozzi, Guglielmo Berchet, Marco Allegri. Venice: Deputazione (R.) veneta di Storia Patria, 1879-1903.

Schumpeter, Joseph A., *Imperialism and Social Classes.* Trans. by Heinz Norden; ed. P. M. Sweezy. New York: Kelley, 1951.

Sella, Domenico, "Les mouvements longs de l'industrie lainière." *Annales Economies Sociétés Civilizations* (1957), pp. 29-45.

————, "Il declino dell'emporio realtino." *La civiltà veneziana nell'età barocca.* Venice: Centro di cultura e civiltà della fondazione Cini, n.d., pp. 99-121.

Seneca, Federico, *Il doge Leonardo Donà: La sua vita e la sua preparazione politica prima del dogado.* Padua: Antenore, 1959.

Stella, Aldo, "La crisi economica veneziana nella seconda metà del secolo xvi," *Archivio Veneto,* LVIII-LIX (1956), pp. 17-69.

Symonds, John Addington, *Renaissance in Italy; The Age of the Despots.* New York: Holt, 1888.

Tabacco, Giovanni, *Andrea Tron (1712-1785) e la crisi dell'aristocrazia senatoria a Venezia.* Trieste: Smolars, 1957.

"Una delle cause della caduta della repubblica veneta," (anon.). Monumenti storici. Miscellanea, Series IV, Vol. IV. Venice: Deputazione (R.) Veneta di Storia Patria, 1887.

Vietti, A., *Il debito pubblico nelle provincie che hanno formato il primo regno d'Italia.* Milan: Quadrio, 1884.

Visconti, Alessandro. *L'Italia nell'epoca della controriforma.* Vol. VI in *Storia d'Italia.* Milan: Mondadori, 1958.

Wiel, Alethea. *The Navy of Venice.* London: Murray, 1910.

Yriarte, Charles E. *La vie d'un patricien de Venise au seizième siècle.* Paris: Plon. 1874.

INDEX

Page numbers set in italics signify most important reference for subject as listed.

149

THE JOHNS HOPKINS UNIVERSITY
STUDIES IN
HISTORICAL AND POLITICAL SCIENCE

❧ ❧ ❧

EIGHTIETH SERIES (1962)

❧ ❧ ❧

THE JOHNS HOPKINS PRESS

BALTIMORE

THE JOHNS HOPKINS UNIVERSITY STUDIES I
HISTORICAL AND POLITICAL SCIENCE

A subscription for the regular annual series is $6.50. Single numbers may be purchased at special prices. A complete list of the series follows.

iii

History of Japanese Paper Currency.
By M. Takai .... O. P.
7. Economics and Politics in Maryland,
1720-1750, and the Public Services of
Daniel Dulany the Elder. By St. G. L.
Sioussat .... O. P.
9-10. Beginnings of Maryland, 1631-
1639. By B. C. Steiner........... O. P.
12. English Statutes in Maryland. By
St. G. L. Sioussat................ O. P.

ENTY-SECOND SERIES (1904)

2. Trial Bibliography of American
Trade-Union Publications, A. By G.
E. Barnett...................... 2.00
4. White Servitude in Maryland, 1634-
1820. By E. I. McCormac......... O. P.
Switzerland at the Beginning of the
Sixteenth Century. By J. M. Vincent. 1.00
7-8. History of Reconstruction in Virginia. By H. J. Eckenrode........ O. P.
10. Foreign Commerce of Japan Since
the Restoration. By Y. Hattori..... 1.25
12. Descriptions of Maryland. By B.
C. Steiner...................... 1.50

ENTY-THIRD SERIES (1905)

2. Reconstruction in South Carolina.
By J. P. Hollis.................. O. P.
4. State Government in Maryland, 1777-
1781. By B. W. Bond, Jr. .... O. P.
5. Colonial Administration Under Lord
Clarendon, 1660-1667. By P. L. Kaye. 2.25
8. Justice in Colonial Virginia. By O.
P. Chitwood.................... O. P.
10. Napoleonic Exiles in America, 1815-
1819. By J. S. Reeves............ O. P.
12. Municipal Problems in Medieval
Switzerland. By J. M. Vincent...... .75

ENTY-FOURTH SERIES (1906)—
Bound Volume .... O. P.

2. Spanish-American Diplomatic Rela-
tions Before 1898. By H. E. Flack.. O. P.
4. Finances of American Trade Unions.
By A. M. Sakolski............... 2.25
5. Diplomatic Negotiations of the
United States with Russia. By J. C.
Hildt 2.50
8. State Rights and Parties in North
Carolina, 1776-1831. By H. M. Wag-
staff 2.25
10. National Labor Federations in the
United States. By William Kirk.... 2.25
12. Maryland During the English Civil
Wars. Part I. By B. C. Steiner.... 1.50

ENTY-FIFTH SERIES (1907)—Bound
Volume .... O. P.

Internal Taxation in the Philippines.
By J. S. Hord.................... .75

2-3. Monroe Mission to France, 1794-
1796. By B. W. Bond, Jr......... 1.75
4-5 Maryland During the English Civil
Wars. Part II. By Bernard C. Steiner. 1.75
6-7. State in Constitutional and International Law. By R. T. Crane....... O. P.
8-9-10. Financial History of Maryland,
1789-1848. By Hugh S. Hanna.... 2.00
11-12. Apprenticeship in American Trade
Unions. By J. M. Motley......... 2.00

TWENTY-SIXTH SERIES (1908)

1-3. British Committees, Commissions,
and Councils of Trade and Planta-
tions, 1622-1675. By C. M. Andrews. O. P.
4-6. Neutral Rights and Obligations in
the Anglo-Boer War. By R. G. Camp-
bell 2.25
7-8. Elizabethan Parish in Its Ecclesiasti-
cal and Financial Aspects. By S. L.
Ware 1.75
9-10. Study of the Topography and Municipal History of Praeneste, A. By
R. V. D. Magoffin................ 1.75
11-12. Beneficiary Features of American
Trade Unions. By J. B. Kennedy.. O. P.

TWENTY-SEVENTH SERIES (1909)

1-2. Self-Reconstruction of Maryland,
1864-1867. By W. S. Myers....... 2.00
3-4-5. Development of the English Law
of Conspiracy. By J. W. Bryan..... 2.50
6-7. Legislative and Judicial History of
the Fifteenth Amendment. By J. M.
Mathews 2.00
8-12. England and the French Revolution,
1789-1797. By W. T. Laprade...... O. P.

TWENTY-EIGHTH SERIES (1910) —
Bound Volume .... O. P.

1. History of Reconstruction in Louisiana.
(Through 1868). By J. R. Ficklen.. O. P.
2. Trade Union Label. By E. R. Spedden 1.75
3. Doctrine of Non-Suability of the State
in the United States. By K. Singewald 2.00
4. David Ricardo: A Centenary Estimate.
By J. H. Hollander.............. O. P.

TWENTY-NINTH SERIES (1911)

1. Maryland Under the Commonwealth:
A Chronicle of the Years 1649-1658.
By B. C. Steiner..Paper 2.50; Cloth 3.00
2. Dutch Republic and the American
Revolution. By Friedrich Edler..... 3.00
3. Closed Shop in American Trade Unions.
By F. T. Stockton................ O. P.

THIRTIETH SERIES (1912)—Bound Vol-
ume .... O. P.

1. Recent Administration in Virginia. By
F. A. Magruder.................. 2.50

vii